Reflections: Poems and Essays

By: Allison Bruning

Mountain Springs House functions only as the book publisher and as such, the ultimate design, content, editorial accuracy, historical accuracy and views expressed or implied in this work are those of the author.

Dedication

To my fans! You are all the best!

To my grandmother, Betty Carr, who always encouraged me to follow my literary dreams.

To my husband, Delfin Espinosa. I love you! You are my best friend. Thank you for supporting me through the mountains and valleys of my writing career.

To Nate Orlowek, thank you for inspiring to search for the truth in history. You have set me on the path that has inspired me to write the unheard stories of the past.

Introduction

Poetry. It is the heart and soul of every writer that pours words onto an empty page. I have been writing poetry since I can remember. Each stroke of my pen, spilling emotions I had hidden deep within. Some I've kept private while others I have made public. I have recorded some of those public poems in this book. I hope you enjoy it.

I have also included some of my essays. I have always been fascinated by the untold stories of history and have included some of those stories in this book. So sit back, relax, and let your mind wonder with me as we explore the "what ifs".

American Confliction

American born.
German bred.
A sailor serving in a war
That I dread.

Adrift at sea
Fighting for my country
Against my parent's family
While citizens at home spit upon me

Conflicted and confused
Terror plagues my dreams
War outside mirrors war within.
Will blood I shed be my kin

Death before me
Persecution behind me
I'm caught in the middle on this desolate sea.
Yet safer here than in my own hometown.

Suspicion abounds
The land of the free
Turns into land of captivity
American citizens trapped in a camp
German heritage their only crime

Does anyone hear - Does anyone care
Lost are the free, lost are the brave
My innocence gone in a sea of uncertainty

Sequoyah: The Man Behind the Legend

Sequoyah. He is as much of a heroic legend among the Cherokee as Tecumseh is for the Shawnee. Like Tecumseh, Sequoyah was a real man who accomplished an extraordinary deed in extraordinary circumstances. When dealing with historical figures who have been lifted up to demi-god status, such as Tecumseh and Sequoyah, there are often more fabricated stories than truths. People tend to forget figures like these men were human beings with faults of their own and human emotions. I often wondered what the thoughts were of such men when faced with the greatest of adversities.

Who Were Sequoyah's Parents?

Sequoyah was born around 1776 in the Cherokee village of Tuskeegee, which was located close to present day Vonore, Tennessee. He was considered a half-breed since his mother was Cherokee and his father was white. Born into two different worlds, Sequoyah's life as a native was riddled with complications. To understand his life we must first understand his parents and the world in which he was born into.

During the French and Indian War (1754-1763), native tribes aided either the British or the French with military support. The first four years of the war the Cherokee had fought along the British, which brought them into many conflicts with the Shawnee who fought on the side of the French. Although the British and Cherokee had joined forces at the beginning of the war both parties held great suspicions against each other that would eventually tear apart their union. Tensions grew between the British settlers and Cherokee until it finally erupted into the Anglo-Cherokee War. The Anglo-Cherokee war, (aka: Cherokee Uprising) lasted from 1758 - 1761. Although the war had ended it didn't mark the end of open hostilities. The French and Indian War was still going on. Just as the French and Indian War had drawn to a close the British colonists were beginning to revolt against their mother country, Great Britain. This rebellion affected all native groups.

Native groups had been trading with Europeans since the early 1600's. It had been over a hundred years of the symbiotic relationship between Europeans and the native populations. The native populations have become so dependent upon European guns and other trade goods in order to survive they had forgotten the ways of their ancestors and were unable to live without European goods. After the British had forced France to abandon their trade with the native populations and leave the area or face military repercussions, the natives who had been dependent upon them had to look for other European traders for their survival. (Point to Ponder: There were some French traders who did live in New Spain at the time and continued to trade with the native groups after the expulsion. They would cross the Mississippi River, sneak into British territory, trade, then high tail back into New Spain where the British could never find them.) At the start of the American Revolution, the Second Continental Congress had addressed the Iroquois Nations asking them to spread this word among the native populations:

We desire you will hear and receive what we have now told you, and that you will open a good ear and listen to what we are now going to say. This is a family quarrel between us and Old England. You Indians are not concerned in it. We don't wish you to take up the hatchet against the king's troops. We desire you to remain at home, and not join on either side, but keep the hatchet buried deep."
—The Second Continental Congress, Speech to the Six Nations, July 13, 1775

The idea of keeping the native populations out of the rebellion was short lived and it wasn't long before the Cherokee had to choose a side as well. Unlike the French and Indian War, the Cherokee chose to fight alongside the Shawnee in support of the British. The Cherokee entered the war in the same year of Sequoyah's birth.

Born Out Of Greatness

Sequoyah's mother, Wut-teh, was the daughter of the Cherokee chief Great Willenawah and his wife Ani-Wa'Di. She was born about 1742 in Tasagi Town, Tennessee. Wut-teh belonged to Red Paint Clan, a medicine society among the Cherokee. She was a member of a prominent, leading Cherokee family. Her two brothers, Tahlonteeske and Kahn-yan-tah-hee, were men of great distinction. Kahn-yan-tah-hee was known as Chota to the British because he was the principal chief of the large Cherokee village bearing the same name. Kahn-yan-tah-hee was called a Beloved Chief by his people. It was his exclusive duty and greatest delight to serve as peace-preserver of his village. Chota was part of the Overhill Cherokee towns, the same group of towns that Sequoyah's father had lived close to during the 1770's. Cherokee heritage is passed down from a child's mother. As such, Sequoyah was taught by the medicine men how to find herbs and plants to heal the sick. Sequoyah was known to white settlers as being an "ingenious natural mechanic" meaning he was very intuitive.

Sequoyah's father, Nathaniel Gist, was the son of the infamous and accomplished frontiersman, surveyor and explorer, Christopher Gist. Christopher Gist is more widely known for his travels with the young George Washington in 1753-1754. George Washington and Christopher Gist had surveyed and mapped portions of the Ohio Wilderness of the Ohio Company.

Nathaniel Gist was born on October 15, 1733 in Baltimore, Maryland. He had two brothers, one of whom was killed at the Battle of King's Mountain in 1780 and four sisters. Nathaniel is sometimes mistaken in historical documents for his uncle Nathaniel Gist, whom was his father's brother and had married his mother's sister. During the French and Indian War, Nathaniel Gist joined his father in Braddock's Expedition, serving as Lieutenant. This is possibly where Nathaniel met Daniel Boone, as Daniel had served as scout and wagon driver for the Braddock's Expedition. After the expedition Nathaniel continued to fight in the French and Indian war protecting settlers against the pro-French natives. In 1757, he was granted the commission of Captain and was given the assignment to lead 200 Cherokee warriors in an auxiliary unit against the French. This was not the first time Nathaniel had encounter the Cherokee. He had been trading with them since he was twenty years old. He led his Cherokee Auxiliary group in the John Forbes campaign where he and his men reoccupied Fort Duchesne. Three years later, just as his father had done with George Washington, Nathaniel travelled into the Ohio Wilderness with Daniel Boone to explore and hunt in the frontier. Nathaniel and Daniel split in their journey, where Nathaniel explored the Cumberland Gap and Daniel headed in the opposite direction. The two never saw each other again in the journey.

A year later, Nathaniel entered the Anglo-Cherokee War, serving as an officer in Adam Steven's Virginia Regiment against the

Cherokees. After the war, he took up employment as a Deputy Indian Trader for the British and settled in the Overhill Cherokee towns along the Little Tennessee River. There he began a romantic relationship with Wut-teh. In March of 1775 he helped negotiate the Treaty of Sycamore Shoals between the Cherokee and the Transylvania Company, whereupon the Cherokee sold a large portion of the lands in Kentucky and northeastern Tennessee to Richard Henderson. During this time the Revolutionary War was just beginning. Nathaniel urged the Cherokees to stay out of the disagreements between the settlers and Great Britain. He felt loyal to the crown because of his position as Deputy Indian Trader. That same year he travelled to West Florida in search of lands that could be awarded to Loyalists (those who were loyal to Great Britain) who were living among the Cherokee. He returned from the trip with British Indian Trader to the Southern Tribes, Henry Stuart. The following year, Wut-teh gave birth to Sequoyah.

Although Nathaniel had warned the Cherokee not to enter into the war, they had already begun to attack patriot settlements before Sequoyah was born. In July of 1776, he accompanied the Cherokee warriors when they attacked the Watauga Settlements. The brutality of the Cherokee warriors against the settlers repulsed Nathaniel. He soon lost interest in staying with his Cherokee wife and son and dreamed of returning to his own people. On January 11, 1777, Nathaniel Gist changed his position in the war and was given commission as colonel in the Continental Army by his father's friend, George Washington. He served in the American Revolutionary War and retired from his army career on January 1, 1783. Sequoyah was seven years old. Yet Nathaniel never returned to his wife and son. Instead, he married Judith Cary Bell that year. The couple had four children together. Nathaniel never forgot Sequoyah. When Sequoyah was an adult he was a Baptist preacher in Kentucky and would often visit his father. Nathaniel and his family accepted him as his son.

Abandoned by his father, raised by his mother during a time of war and chaos, Sequoyah's early years were anything but pleasant.

The Early Years

Before Sequoyah's father abandoned his pregnant and devoted Cherokee wife, he had predicted to her she was carrying his son. His father had abandoned the family before Wut-teh gave birth to Sequoyah. No one knows exactly how the boy became to be known as Sequoyah among the Cherokee. Some speculate his mother named him this because it means "he guessed it," relating to Nathanial's speculation about the gender of his son. Another explanation of the name, which is more widely accepted, lies in an accident Sequoyah had as a young boy. The young Sequoyah went pig hunting one day and had a hunting accident that left him permanently crippled in one of his legs. From that day on he was nicknamed Sequoyah "pig's feet" and used the name until he reached adulthood, where he adopted the name George Gist. Raised by his Cherokee mother, Sequoyah never adopted any of his father's white culture. He never learned to read, write or speak the white language nor accept their religion. Wut-teh was a powerful medicine woman and had proven herself in battle plenty of times before she met Sequoyah's father. She made certain to teach her son in the old ways of the Cherokee people in the mountains of Tennessee.

Sequoyah wasn't an easy child to teach. His inability to use part of his crippled leg made it hard for him run, walk, jump, etc. He lived a solitary life with his mother who allowed him to help her with the women's work of gardening and helping with the cattle. Wut-teh was a successful trader who had a considerable amount of cattle and horses. She would often trade her excess produce and furs with the white settlers and traders. Thus Sequoyah was introduced early on to the white nation but never accepted any of their culture. Despite having grey eyes and a sallow complexion, the Cherokee considered Sequoyah to be full-blooded. Sequoyah grew up knowing he was of mixed blood but never accepted it nor wanted to explore his father's culture until his adult life. He had two brothers, Tobacco Will; a blacksmith in Alabama who signed the Cherokee Constitution; and Dutch, the Old Settler Chief.

Sequoyah was often ridiculed by his peers. Despite his deformity, he strove to be accepted by them as any normal boy would. He knew he would never be the fastest runner or the best warrior but he had to try. Sequoyah preserved and acquired the skills he would need in battle and on a daily basis. He was taught all the skills he would need to be a successful Cherokee man. Aside from his cripple leg, Sequoyah's own mind often held him back in his Cherokee education. Sequoyah was a very intelligent boy but he was also a dreamer and very moody. He hated war and did not like to participate in the games boys were supposed to play in order to build up their skills for war. One can only imagine his frustrations with his leg probably instigated his dislike of sports and war. Like Daniel Boone, he would oftentimes escape from his daily rigors into the backwoods. Alone, the genius boy would build complex miniature houses made of stick and mud. I can only imagine the frustrations Wut-teh must have had with her son! Wut-teh died in 1800.

The Artisan

After her death in the beginning of the 19th century, Sequoyah had a hard time dealing with his mother's death and soon began to drown his sorrows with alcohol. He neglected his farm and the trade business, all of which he had inherited from his mother. Sequoyah had more days he was drunk than sober. When he ran out of money to buy alcohol in large quantities he began to plead with his friends for their aide. He led such a reckless life many of his friends began to call him "drunken Sequoyah." One by one his friends abandoned him.

After a while, Sequoyah began to realize the destructive path he was creating for his own life. He made the decision to no longer live the life of an alcoholic. Sequoyah was able to do this by taking up a new interest, blacksmithing. Sequoyah had noticed as the white settlers moved closer to the lands in which his people lived, there were new iron implements being introduced in the trade markets. Eating utensils, hammers, tongs, and other objects made of iron would eventually break. Like other native groups who didn't have the white man's technology, his people would have to depend upon the European traders to provide and repair the new objects. Sequoyah began to think, "Why couldn't the Cherokee learn to create and repair these implements themselves? Why should the Cherokee have to depend upon the white man for something they could do for themselves if they had the right equipment and the knowledge?" Sequoyah quickly abandoned his alcoholism in order to bring the art of blacksmithing to his people. He built his own bellows, forge fires, hammers, tongs, and drills. His reputation as a drunkard was soon replaced with a reputation of a superb blacksmith. People came from all over just to buy the arrows, knives, hoes and other implements he made. His trade house soon became not only a place to trade but a gathering place for the Cherokee people. He stopped selling alcohol and greatly encouraged the Cherokee to never allow it into their population. Sequoyah's efforts were affluent in the passing of the first prohibition law ever created in the United States, which was not done by the United States but by the Cherokee. While he was blacksmithing he also built up his trade business. Sequoyah would travel far and wide to trade furs he would bring back to his own trade house. In his travels, he often encountered several white people.

After he perfected his blacksmithing skills, Sequoyah began to notice his people were sill dependent upon the white traders. The Cherokee were fond of the silver ornaments such as arm-bands, broaches, and bracelets. If he could become a blacksmith then why couldn't he become a silversmith, too? Once again, Sequoyah's brilliant mind went to work. He taught himself silversmithing. His reputation soon spread even farther. He not only crafted silver ornaments but also combined his blacksmithing and silversmithing together by creating bridles and other pieces with silver laced in them. People came from all around to buy his silver laced bridles and bits. As he traded with the white man, he began to realize his blacksmithing and silversmithing was an art form. He was selling his art without having his mark on them! He sought out one of his friends to help him, a half-blooded Cherokee chief known as Charles Hicks. Since Charles knew how to write in English, Sequoyah asked him to teach him how to write his name. Charles agreed. Instead of writing the name Sequoyah, Charles wrote Sequoyah's white name and misspelled the last name, simply writing George Guess and not Gist. Sequoyah thank his friend, took the written form and made a die cast of the name. Every piece Sequoyah made in his blacksmithing and silversmithing since then have had the name GEORGE GUESS stamped to it. Who would have known a piece from the same time period with that name upon it would have been made by Sequoyah's hands? The Father of the Cherokee language.

Talking Leaves

Sequoyah's trade house was often used as a gathering place for the Cherokee. In his travels he often encountered the white man and had seen how they communicate with "talking leaves" Talking leaves were the pages of writing, such as letters and books that the white man used to communicate with one another. Many of the Cherokee believed the use of these items was a form of witchcraft. But Sequoyah, who couldn't read nor write in English, was intrigued by them. In 1809, a group of Cherokee captured a white man who had a crumbled up letter in his pocket. The Cherokee had demanded their prisoner read the letter to them but he had refused. Fearing it was a message from the Great Spirit, they quickly took the "talking leaf" to Sequoyah. The mysterious writing had intrigued Sequoyah. For weeks and months he studied the letter. Although he couldn't read nor write in English, he sought out the white man's books and letters in order to study them. Sequoyah became obsessed with the white man's talking leaves. None of the leaves would talk to him but that didn't discourage him. One day, as he was relaxing with his friends, the topic of conversation turned to white man's talking leaves. They began to discuss whether or not the white man's talking leaves were superior to their own communication methods. Sequoyah had advocated the white man possessed more power over the Cherokee by stating, "Much that red men know, they forget," he stated. "They have no way to preserve it. White men make what they know fast on paper, like catching the wild panther and taming it." This did not sit well with his friends. Many of them ridiculed him. The conversation ended but Sequoyah's dream did not.

For three years Sequoyah worked on developing the Cherokee alphabet until the War of 1812. The War of 1812 pitted the nearly formed United States against Great Britain. Once again, the native population took sides. The Cherokee were of no exception. They fought alongside Andrew Jackson against the British. Despite the deformity of his leg, Sequoyah enlisted at Turkeytown on October 7, 1813 and participated in the Battle of Tallaschatche. Three weeks after his three month tour of service was over, Sequoyah reenlisted. He fought in the Battle of Horseshoe Bend on March 27, 1814. The Cherokee were vital in helping the United States defeat the British allied Creek Native Americans. During the war, Sequoyah began to pay more attention to the "talking leaves". He and his fellow Cherokee warriors were dishearten in that the white man could communicate with their loved ones through the use of the talking leaves. Without being able to read and write, his people were left without the ability to communicate with their loved ones for the entire sixty days they were at war. The disappointments in his fellow Cherokee's faces only further encouraged Sequoyah into developing the Cherokee alphabet.

After the war, Sequoyah went back to his trade house and began to work in earnest at developing a written language for his people. In 1815, he fell in love with a woman of the Bird Clan named Sally Waters. At first, they were deeply in love with each other and had four children together. But as time went on she grew tired with her husband's constant drawing and pleaded for him to abandon them. Sequoyah refused. He wasn't just drawing. He was developing a set of pictographs. One day, Sally took all of his work and burned everything. Despite her efforts to destroy his work, he pressed on and started again. Sequoyah had already committed each symbol to his memory so it was easy for him to start over. He left his wife and children and went to a secluded cabin where he could work in privacy. Despite his best efforts to get away from the constant intolerance of his peers, his disappearance only caused him more heartache. While he was gone, his Cherokee neighbors burned his house down along with the wooden tiles he had carved. Luckily Sally and the children were not injured. Then they ransacked his private cottage and captured him. The vigilantes punished him for his witchcraft by branding his head and back, cut off his ears and cut his fingers back to the second joint. Sequoyah returned to his wife and children but did not stop with the development of the Cherokee language. He began to teach his young daughter, Ah-yo-ka, how to read and write the glyphs he had already created.

In 1817, a warrant was issued out of Knoxville for his arrest on charges of witchcraft. Here is a copy of the warrant:

"*You will confer a favor on certain citizens of the Cherokee Nation, by giving publicity of the following description of a Cherokee, who committed a crime of witchcraft, and murder to one of our citizens on the 22nd December last. This man is called by the white people, Sequoyah. He is about 6 feet high, upwards of 50 years old; his appearance is rather rough, and attempts some times to speak English; his face is somewhat slender, and several weeks ago, he was disfigured by cutting his ears and fingers off by another Indian. He, I believe, has a circle on his forehead, artificially placed by burning. He has sparse whiskers, most of them bear frost of age. His hair, I believe is about shoulder length.*"

Sequoyah knew he could not be executed without a hearing, since the 1811 Cherokee constitution forbid such an act. But he wasn't about to allow the Cherokee to capture him, not after what they had done to him already. In 1818, he moved his family from Alabama to Arkansas where he not only continued his work but conducted business in a salt production and blacksmith operation.

Who is the real John Wilkes Booth?

John Wilkes Booth is known to most people through history as a treacherous man who murdered Abraham Lincoln and died after being captured at Garrett's Farm. But what if history got it all wrong? What if John Wilkes Booth had evaded capture and lived to a ripe old age? These are the questions that have plagued the mind of historian Nate Orlowek and his associates. After years of research Nate Orlowek had concluded, "There is tremendous physical evidence that proved beyond a doubt that John Wilkes Booth, in reality, was not killed by the Federal Government Officers as they claimed. In fact, he lived until January 13th, 1903, when he died in Enid, Oklahoma territory." But how can this be? Why would our government claim they had killed John Wilkes Booth only over a hundred years later we learn that this wasn't the case?

I had first learned of historian Nate Orlowek and his research in 1992 while watching Unsolved Mysteries. A few days later, our English professor assigned us to write a research paper on an American president. I decided I wanted to write about the death of John Wilkes Booth. I immediately contacted the show. They put me in contact with Mr. Orlowek. The historian and I talked for hours and he sent me copies of his research. I wrote my research paper based on his evidence and concluded that John Wilkes Booth did not die at Garrett Farm but lived to old age in Enid, Oklahoma Territory under the alias of David E. George. But what would also drive me to the same conclusion as Nate Orlowek and why do others believe him as well?

On April 14, 1865, President Abraham Lincoln and his wife attended the play, Our American Cousin, at Ford's Theatre with Major Henry Rathbone and his fiancée, Clara Harris. Below the Presidential Box, the theatre was filled to capacity with 1,700 people in attendance. President Lincoln and his wife had arrived late to the play. After their arrival they sat very close to each other and enjoyed the play while holding hands. It had been the first time in a very long time Abraham Lincoln had been happy. Sometime during the intermission, John

Frederick Parker, who was supposed to be standing guard outside the presidential box, had left the theatre to have a drink at a nearby tavern with the president's footman and coachman. John Wilkes Booth, who was so familiar with Ford's Theatre that he had a permanent mailbox at the establishment, entered the theatre through the back door with the help of a stagehand who recognizes him. Booth proceeds to make his way towards the Presidential Box. The audience members who see Booth assume he is at the theatre to call upon the president and pay no attention to the famous actor. At 10:15 the third act of the play began. John Frederick Parker never returned to his post outside the Presidential Box. Five minutes later, Mrs. Lincoln leaned into her husband and whispered, "What will Miss Harris think of my hanging on to you so?" Her husband replied, "She won't think anything about it." As fate would have it, these were to be Abraham Lincoln's last words.

Dr. Charles Brainerd Todd ,a Navy surgeon who was stationed on the US monitor vessel Montauk and was in attendance that night, stated in his eye witness statement. "About 10:25 pm, a man came in and walked slowly along the side on which the "Pres" box was and I heard a man say, "There's Booth" and I turned my head to look at him. He was still walking very slow and was near the box door when he stopped, took a card from his pocket, wrote something on it, and gave it to the usher who took it to the box. In a minute the door was opened and he walked in."

After John Wilkes Booth had gained entry into the hallway that lead to the Presidential Box he bared the door with a wooden stick so no one could gain entry. He proceeded to the second door, peered into the peep hole he had carved into the door earlier that day, and waited. John Wilkes Booth knew the play by heart and had planned to assassinate the president at the perfect time. It was now Act 3 Scene 2. Booth waited for the actor to deliver the funniest line of the show and then the audience to respond. Just as the audience laughter lifted into the air and President Lincoln leaned over gazing towards someone he recognized to the lower left of the house floor, Booth entered the box, aimed his single shot Derringer gun on the president head and shot him at point blank range behind the left ear. The president fell forward into this wife's arms. When Major Rathbone heard the shot beside he had risen from his chair and tried to capture Booth. Booth grabbed a knife, sliced the major's arm down to the bone and tried to jump over the box rail. Rathbone grabbed Booth again. Booth stabbed Rathbone in the chest then leapt over the rail. As he jumped, one of his spurs caught on the Treasury flag that was draped across the front of the president's box. He landed hard on the stage, breaking his left leg. Booth rose and acted as if he was part of the play. He raised his knife, yelling to the audience, "The South is avenged" in Latin then ran out of the stage door. The audience only realized Booth was not part of the show when Mrs. Lincoln's and Clara Harris' screams were heard while Major Rathbone yelled "Stop that man!"

After Booth left, several army surgeons went to the box to give all the help they could. But when they got up there it was too late. There was no hope for they knew the blow was fatal. The bullet had entered the head and rested behind the president's left eye. Because of his great length, the doctors agreed to have the dying president moved to a house across the street. President Lincoln died April 16, 1865 at 7:22 in the morning.

At the death of their great leader, the people all over the country were in a state of shock and mourning. The North was in chaos after hearing the disastrous news. There had been no sleep that night nor had there been any business openings. The people, through anger and rage, mobbed cities and soldiers even killed those who had made fun of the late president. People's houses were decorated in black and on that Easter (known as Black Easter) people went to church dressed in black. If they weren't, they were considered traitors and were either shot or tortured by those who found out. The country lay in ruins and the people demanded justice. The United States government decided to give the people what they wanted. They interviewed several of the witnesses to determine the identity of the assassin. Finally after hours of investigation they had compiled a warrant for John Wilkes Booth with the following description; 1) Brown hair 2) wild eyed 3) 5 feet 9 inches 4) slender built 5) high forehead 6) black eyes and 7) heavy black mustache. The government then ordered two thousand Union soldiers to give chase.

After President Lincoln was shot, the army had been ordered to set up roadblocks on all possible escape routes out of the city, in hopes to capture the assailant. But this didn't stop John Wilkes Booth and his co-conspirator, David Herold. Booth and Herold gave the guards a fake password then escaped out of the city by midnight. The two went to a tavern owned by Mrs. Surratt. They had a few drinks, got Booth's field glasses, left the tavern and travelled south. By the next morning, they had arrived to a house owned by Dr. Samuel Mudd. The doctor had not recognized the two men and decided to set Booth's leg. He laid Booth on a bed in the back of the room, cut off his boot and set the broken left bone. Booth slept until morning then headed further south. Five days later, the military arrested Mudd for providing assistance to Booth. Although he denied knowing who the man was, he was tried and convicted of treason. In 1883, he died at the age of 49.

The greed caused by the reward money offered for Booth's capture only slowed down his capture. According to history, John Wilkes Booth and David Herold had crossed the Rappahannock River in Virginia via a ferry operated by Willie Jett. Booth and Herold had entertained a lively conversation with the operator claiming they had just killed the president. Colonel Everton J. Conger and two other investigators approached Jett after the conspirators left concerning the whereabouts of the assassins. Jett told them Booth and Herold were hiding in Richard Garrett's barn. Conger then leads his troop to the barn and trapped the two men.

The night at Garrett's barn must have been exciting to the Union soldiers there. They were about to capture John Wilkes Booth. The soldiers had been ordered to take Booth alive. The soldiers aimed their guns at the barn and ordered everyone out. Conger yelled he would give the men five minutes to remove themselves from the barn or he would smoke them out. David Herold left the barn and surrendered to the troops. Herold informed the officers that Booth was not in the barn but rather a man named Boyd. Remember that name as we will come back to it. When Booth did not accompany him, Conger ordered his men to set the barn on fire. They had been ordered to take Booth alive. Conger had hoped to smoke the assassin out of his hiding place. As one of the soldiers lit the place on fire, he could see a man inside the barn on crutches. Booth was shot in the neck by Sergeant Boston Corbett as the blaze burned. The soldiers carried his body out of the barn. Booth had repeated several times for them to kill him afterwards but they did not. While Booth lay dying Conger took Booth's notebook and belongings as evidence then raced to Washington to proclaim they had killed the assassin. The soldiers laid him on the porch of Richard Garrett's house and waited for him to die. He died several hours later. The following morning his body was transported to the Washington Naval Yard where it was laid out on a plank on the US Montauk for autopsy. There was a formal hearing End of story, right? Not if you believe Nate Orlowek.

According to Nate Orlowek and several of his colleagues, Booth had been at the barn earlier, but wasn't there any longer by the time the soldiers arrived. Remember when I told you Herold had claimed the man wasn't Booth but was a man by the name of Boyd? During the

April 14, 1865 trial of the conspirators, Lieutenant Edward Doherty, who had been at the barn testified,

(Herold)"Who is that that has been shot in the in the barn?"
"Why," I (Doherty) said "you know well who it is."
Said he (Herold), "No, I do not; he told me his name was Boyd."
Said I, (Doherty)"It is Booth, and you know it."
Said he, (Herold) "No, I did not know that it was Booth."

Doherty was not the only one to have claimed the body that day was not John Wilkes Booth. There are three other eyewitnesses that also support this claim.

- Mr. Wilson D. Kenzie – He was one of the members of the 16th N.Y. Calvary who rode up to the barn shortly after the death of Booth. He gave the following statement on June 19, 1922."This fellow's a red-headed Virginian... he was a red head and had read hair. There was no chance of mistake....One of the three officers of high rank seized the blanket and shouted to me 'Don't you repeat that'....My company commander, Lt. Morris, husband of the niece of Secretary Stanton, warned me to keep my mouth shut."
- Basil Moxley – He was a former doorman at the Ford's Opera house in Baltimore and was one of the pallbearers at the 1869 funeral of John Wilkes Booth. On June 6, 1903, he told the Baltimore News American that the 1869 burial of John Wilkes Booth was a "mock funeral". He claimed that the corpse had "red or reddish hair".
- Lieutenant William C. Allen of the U.S. Secret Service told his wife Hannah, who then told Rufus Woods, a journalist, that her husband had seen the body in Virginia. He said the body had "auburn or chestnut hair."

- John Wilkes Booth's body had been secretly examined on the Montauk shortly after his death. A photograph of Booth's body had been taken by he well-known Washington photographer, Alexander Gardner and his assistant. The photograph was sent directly to the War Department and has since vanished. Surgeon General Joseph K. Barnes and Dr. Joseph Janvier Woodward were ordered to conduct the autopsy. Dr. Barnes wrote in a statement to Secretary Stanton on April 27, 1865.

Sir,

I have the honor to report that in compliance with your orders, assisted by Dr. Woodward, USA, I made at 2 PM this day, a postmortem examination of the body of J. Wilkes Booth, lying on board the Monitor Montauk off the Navy Yard.

The left leg and foot were encased in an appliance of splints and bandages, upon the removal of which, a fracture of the fibula (small bone of the leg) 3 inches above the ankle joint, accompanied by considerable ecchymosis, was discovered.

The cause of death was a gunshot wound in the neck - the ball entering just behind the sterno-cleido muscle - 2 1/2 inches above the clavicle - passing through the bony bridge of fourth and fifth cervical vertebrae - severing the spinal chord (sic) and passing out through the body of the sterno-cleido of right side, 3 inches above the clavicle.

Paralysis of the entire body was immediate, and all the horrors of consciousness of suffering and death must have been present to the assassin during the two hours he lingered.

Upon completion of their report the physicians removed third, fourth and fifth vertebra from Booth's body. These are housed at National Museum of Health and Medicine at the Walter Reed Army Medical Center. Booth's body was buried Green Mount Cemetery. What if the examining physicians were wrong in their report? They were not the only people who had access to the body that day. There had been several people who had been called in to identify the body but according to Nate Orlowek these witnesses hardly knew who John Wilkes Booth was.

Doctor May was a physician who had looked at the body and made a statement to the government. In his statement, he states that body had a "freckled complexion and a broken right leg." A broken right leg? I did not make a mistake here. If you recall Booth had broken his left leg not his right one. Also look to the description of the warrant. Booth did not have a freckled complexion or red hair. John Shumaker, the United States General Counsel to the Department of the Army in the early 1900's had written, "The evidence put forth by the government to support the conclusion that the body was that of John Wilkes Booth was so insubstantial that it would not stand up in a court of law."

If the body was not of John Wilkes Booth then what happened to him?

The idea of Booth's escape from death is not a new one. Such ideas have surfaced in 1898 with reports of John Wilkes Booth making his way to South America. In 1903, reports once again surfaced of Booth's great escape. On January 13, 1903, in Enid, Oklahoma Territory, a man named David E. George committed suicide. George had made a deathbed confession to his landlady that he was in reality John Wilkes Booth. This wasn't the first time George had made that confession. In 1871 or 1872, George had arrived to Tennessee under the name of John Booth. He was quiet mannered and well groomed. He worked as a carpenter. John told everyone he was a distant cousin of the infamous actor. John courted Louisa Payne for a short time them married her.

On their marital night he confessed to his beloved that he had married her under a false identity and that his real name was John Wilkes Booth. A devout Christian woman, she persuaded her husband to marry her under his real name. There is a marriage record in Franklin County, Tennessee that shows John Wilkes Booth signature. John Wilkes Booth had shown his nine –year- old stepson the scar on his left leg from where he had broken his leg in the fall from the balcony. He told the youngster if he ever told anyone he has seen it then he would kill him. Louisa would bathe Booth's leg in hot water to relieve the pain. In July of 1872, the three of them moved to Memphis, Tennessee where Booth was expecting a large sum of money for killing President Lincoln. Booth rented a few rooms from a hotel then got a job in a factory. According to a 1938 article in the Nashville Banner by Florence Wilson, "Booth returned home in a cab greatly excited and told his wife he would have to leave home...He dressed himself in his best clothes, packed a few belongings, and left." Booth promised his wife and son he would keep in touch. Louisa was with child and a few months later gave birth to John Wilkes Booth's daughter. She named the child, Laura Ida Elizabeth Booth. Louisa died five years later. On her deathbed she told her daughter John Wilkes Booth was her father.

David E. George resurfaces in 1872 as John St. Helens in Grandbury, Texas.

John Saint Helens was very ill and called his good friend, Finis L. Bates to his deathbed in order to make a confession. According to Finis L. Bates' book, "The Escape and Suicide of John Wilkes Booth" published in 1907, St. Helens said, ""I am dying. My name is John Wilkes Booth, and I am the assassin of President Lincoln." St. Helens was struggling to maintain consciousness and did not go into much detail. After St. Helens recovered from his illness he sat down with Bates and gave more details of his escape. St. Helens claimed Vice President Andrew Johnson had conceived the assignation plot. He had been able to escape out of Washington, D.C. after he had killed Lincoln because the Vice President had given him the code word (remember in the beginning when I had told you Booth had given the guards the code word so he could get out of town). He claimed he didn't know who the man was that died in the barn that day but suspected it had been the man he had sent to retrieve his belongings. Not only had St. Helens told his friend details about the escape that only John Wilkes Booth would know but he also told him intimate details about the Booth family. After he told his story to Bates, St. Helens left town. Nate Orlowek stated, "This man, if he wasn't John Wilkes Booth, it's pretty darn amazing that he knew all these things."

After confessing to the landlady his true identity, David E. George committed suicide in 1903 by drinking arsenic. George had on his person papers directing that his friend Finis Bates be contacted upon his death. When Bates arrived to Enid, he encountered locals proclaiming George had been John Wilkes Booth. Bates went to the house and immediately recognized the body of John Saint Helens. Bates left the body at the funeral home then returned to Memphis. David E. George's body was mummified in 1911. After Bates death in 1923, the mummy travelled from circus to circus. Everybody wanted to see the mummy. Despite its popularity, the mummy began to be associated with a curse. Seven circus owners who had the mummy on display were financially ruined and eight people died in a train wreck that the mummy was travelling in. In 1931, eight years after Bates death, the mummy was handed over to panel of medical experts in Chicago to be examined. The physicians concluded there was considerable evidence on the mummy to support the claim. The mummy had 1) a scarred right eyebrow that arched upwards, 2) a broken right thumb, and 3) a broken left leg. All were known to be on John Wilkes Booth body. The mummy was last seen on display in 1976 then disappeared. "You don't even need to believe that David E. George was Booth to believe that Booth got away," Nate Orlowek once stated.

Booth family lore also supports that John Wilkes Booth was not in Garrett's Barn when the soldiers arrived. In the 1990's Virginia Kline and her daughter, Joanne Hulme teamed up with Nate Orlowek and his associates to research into the death of John Wilkes Booth. Joanne wrote in March of 2012, "At no time did any of John Wilkes Booth's family identify the body at Garrett's farm; not on the Montague, not at Weaver's Funeral Home, and not at the barn. The government could have brought the Booth family forth, but chose not to. Joseph Booth,

John's brother, said numerous times that neither he nor Edwin Booth ever identified the body." A majority of the Booth family does not believe John Wilkes Booth died in the barn. Both Edwin Booth, John's brother, and their mother, Mary Ann Holmes' Booth, had claimed they had personally entertained a visit with John Wilkes Booth after his alleged death in 1865.

On May 17, 1995, Lois W. Rathbun, Booth's great great grandniece, and Virginia Eleanor Humbrecht Kline who is Booth's first cousin, twice removed, petitioned the Circuit Court for Baltimore City to exhume the body of John Wilkes Booth. They had claimed they desired the exhumation in order to identify who was buried in John Wilkes Booth's grave. The Greenmont Cemetery opposed the Booth relatives and presented documented evidence of Booth's capture and death via the Surrett Society. The cemetery claimed John Wilkes Booth's mother didn't want any fanfare over his death. She bought land from Greenmont and ordered the cemetery to bury her son in an unmarked grave. Greenmont claimed they do not know for certain where John Wilkes Booth is buried but have a pretty good idea of the location. If their suspicions are correct then there may be three infant siblings buried in a casket on top of his. They argued if the courts were to allow the Booth family to exhume the body they would inappropriately disturb the infant's bodies. Even if the family was able to convince the judge to exhume Booth's body it would be hard to positively identify it. Greenmont claims the plot where Booth's body may lie has undergone extensive water damage that could have affected his remains. Experts testified that with the amount of time the body has been lying in the ground any test results would be inaccurate. Forget dental records or DNA as well. There is a lack of dental records during that time. DNA testing would only be viable if the Booth descendants were closely related to John Wilkes Booth such as a brother, parent or child. After hearing testimony from experts and examining historical documentation of Booth's capture and death, Judge Joseph H. H. Kaplan ruled against the Booth relatives and ordered the body not to be exhumed.

Nate Orlowek hasn't given up. There may be another way to test whether the man buried in Greenmont Cemetery is the real John Wilkes Booth or not. Remember those vertebra pieces that I had mentioned were removed from John Wilkes Booth's body at autopsy? Well over a hundred years old, they are still housed within the National Museum of Health and Medicine. Family members want to exhume the body of Edwin Booth, John Wilkes Booth's brother, and compare his DNA with a DNA sample from the vertebra. Despite the family's best intentions the museum does not want the vertebra to be touched. Museum officials claim taking a sample could possibly destroy the specimen. Historians disagree stating that an accurate sampling would not destroy the specimen if a tiny drill was used. But the museum isn't budging. They believe the possible harm that could be done outweighs the need to learn the truth about who is buried in Booth's grave. Once again the family is hitting the proverbial legal wall.

Who is the real John Wilkes Booth?

The Rose

She bloomed today
But just today
Then came the rain.

With a thorn in her side
The sun was just over the hill
Calling her name

Ache and pain
Pain and ache
She wanted to be free from it all

Then came the sun
With its bright warm heat
And she bloomed…
And she bloomed…
And she bloomed…
Until the next passing rain.

The rose never dies
It will survive
A beauty so bright
With a thorn in its side.

Can't They See?

Can't they see the athlete?
Can't they see the writer?
Can't they see the student?
Why is it they can't see me?

Can they see my stress?
Can they see the freedom?
Can they see my achievements?
Or do they only see my failures?
I wonder, what do they see?

Can they see my pain?
Can they see my healthy disposition?
When will they ever see me?

Can they see the loyal friend?
Can they see my enemies?
Why do they not see?

Can he see his faithful wife?
Can she see her loving daughter?
How can they know me if they can't see me?

The Jew Behind the Revolutionary Money: Haym Soloman

At the start of the American Revolutionary War, Great Britain had obtained the rank as a global military and economical superpower. Great Britain had perfected its military strength by fighting the Nine Years War (1688-97), the War of Spanish Succession (1702-13), the War of Austrian Succession (1739-48), and the Seven Years War (1756-63). Now her rebellious colonies in the New World were starting another war. There were several factors that led up to the American Revolutionary War. One of the key issues was financial.

From 1733 to 1763, Great Britain operated economically on the mercantile system. Under this system colonists were forbidden to trade with any nation other than Great Britain. The goal of the system was to make the British Empire and her government rich. The colonists viewed this regulation as limiting their own finances. France, Spain, and other countries had colonies in the New World and had their own trade routes as well. To ensure the colonists complied with the mercantile system, Great Britain enacted the Navigation Acts. The Navigation Acts blocked colonial trade with the Dutch, French, and Spanish. The colonists tried their best to avoid the acts. The Navigation Acts were just one of many ways Great Britain limited the financial resources of the colonies.

During the Seven Year's War, Great Britain did not expect the colonists to generate enough of an income to provide financial resources to the monarchy. At the conclusion of the war, Great Britain changed their view on using colonial finances to relieve the national debt the war had caused. The monarchy had spent 200,000 pounds annually in order to protect the colonists and the West Indies from Spanish and French invasions. To meet the demand, British Parliament increased colonial taxes and created new acts of taxation over the years. Back in the colonies, the colonists were infuriated. Most people believe the colonists were upset due to the raise in taxes. It was never the raise in taxes that had upset our forefathers but that there was taxation without representation. The colonists felt they should have representation in British Parliament. British Parliament disagreed. By not allowing the colonists to have a say over matters concerning the colonies, parliament was displaying who was really in charge of the colonies. London replied to the colonists' request for representation, stating the colonists had virtual representation. Virtual representation stated members of Parliament spoke on behalf of all British subjects, not just the ones who had elected them. Since the colonists were British subjects, they had representation. Parliament's position in the matter had critics on both sides of the Atlantic Ocean. In March of 1766, British Parliament had tried to settle the matter by passing the Declaration Act. The Declaration Act declared parliament had full power and control to make whatever laws it had deemed necessary for all the colonies in the New World.

Although there were a series of skirmishes up and down the American coastline, the Revolutionary War didn't official begin until April 19, 1775, with "The Shot Heard Around The World." At the advent of the Revolutionary War, Great Britain lost control of all colonial trade. The colonists were quick to abolish the restrictions their mother country had placed upon them. With the new-found freedoms to trade with whomever the colonists pleased, the colonial trade market flourished. The market also flourished with the help of American pirates stealing resources from British merchant vessels.

The Cost of War

The British had believed the colonial rebellion would be short-lived. But the colonists were determined to win their freedoms and birth a nation. The war for independence lasted 8 years and 137 days, ending on September 3, 1783. The drawn out war had nearly bankrupt both sides of the conflict. The financial resources of the colonies began to deteriorate following their victory at the Battle of Saratoga on October 17, 1777. Up until this time the thirteen states did not financially support congress. Each state had its own currency that had to compete with other currencies. To make matters worse, British spies had infiltrated the colonies and had begun to distribute counterfeit colonial dollars in order to destroy the colonial economy. The British efforts had been successful in causing a rapid depreciation in the value of colonial money. The war had caused a blow to the colonial market as well with inflation, destruction of property, and the deaths of able-bodied men.

The British also attacked American vessels and confiscated any goods that they were transporting, claiming the cargo as British property. Any profits that were made by colonial merchants were sent to help fund the war efforts. A popular saying back then summed the situation well, "anything of little value is not worth a continental." By 1780, congress had released $400 million in paper money to the colonial troops. Congress had tried to help the economic situation by imposing economic reforms that they had hoped would end the inflation. Their efforts failed. It quickly became apparent to our young nation that they were going to need financial support.

An Answered Prayer - Haym Solomon

Haym Solomon was born on April 7, 1740, in Leszo, Poland to Shepardi Jewish parents from Portugal. Haym spent much of his life traveling around Western Europe and England. Although he learned Hebrew in his youth, his adventures granted him the ability to learn a variety of languages. His fluency in a number of languages served him well. In 1770, Haym returned to Poland where he stayed until the Polish partition. He was forced to flee for his life. Haym immigrated to New York in 1772, where through his education and his fluency ability to speak ten languages, he became a successful merchant and dealer of foreign securities. He became friends with Alexander MacDougall, who was the leader of the New York Sons of Liberty. Through their acquaintance, Haym was introduced to the secret revolutionary organization and became a member. This was a bold move for Haym to make, in that New York was the central hub of British power in the colonies and he was already doing business with wealthy loyalists (those who are loyal to Great Britain). When the American Revolutionary War broke out in New York, Haym had already secured a contract to supply the patriot troops in central New York. During the Great Fire of New York on September 9, 1776, Haym Solomon was arrested by British authorities on grounds of espionage. He was imprisoned and tortured on a British vessel for eighteen months. The British noticed Haym's ability to fluently speak 10 languages. They offered him a pardon if he would serve as a translator for their dealings with the Hessian mercenaries. Haym agreed. Instead of aiding the British, he used his skills to help other prisoners escape and he encouraged the Hessians to desert their plans to aid the British. He went back to his business and continued to aid the patriots. In September of 1778, Haym was arrested again by the British for his pro-revolutionary activities. The British charged him with treason and sentenced him to death by hanging. With the help of his friends, he was able to escape. He fled with his family to the patriot capital of Pennsylvania, where he arrived penniless. Haym immediately went back to work and built up his business. Haym continued to aid the patriots.

In Pennsylvania, Congress appointed him as Broker to the Office of Finance for the United States of America. He negotiated many loans from Holland and France for the colonies, never taking a single commission. France appointed him as the Treasurer of the French Army in America. He was able to maintain his personal business transactions and his interest-free loans to various members of the Continental Congress, such as James Madison and James Wilson, while he worked for France and Congress. He fed starving patriot soldiers and commanders. He never sought repayment. Haym became so well known for his financial backing of the revolutionary movement that one revolutionary leader wrote in his journal, "When money was needed for the Revolutionary War, you went to Haym Salomon." Without Haym's backing, the Battle of Yorktown would never have occurred. George Washington and Count de Rochambeau had decided to take their armies up the Hudson Highlands to Yorktown in order to deliver a final blow to the British. The generals determined it would cost $20,000 to finance the campaign. The problem was both Washington and Congress were broke. George Washington ordered Morris, "Send for Haym Salomon." Haym raised the $20,000 and handed it over to George Washington. After the Battle of Yorktown, the British surrendered. Without Haym Solomon, we would not have won the war. Haym Solomon died penniless in 1785. His modern descendants have recently tried to claim compensation from the American government for close to $683,000, which they claim the government owes Haym. Since there are little to no records in existence for personal and government loans Haym had issued, there is no evidence to support their claims. The government has not released any funds to Haym Solomon's descendants.

Ka-Ching!

Smell the fragrant honeysuckle of money.
Taste its sweet honey
Don't you love the feel of a brand new bill?
Oh, President Franklin,
how I do love you.
Ka-Ching!

Glistening diamonds
Calling my name.
What's this?
She has a bigger wedding ring?
Well that won't do.
I have to buy.
Ka-Ching!

Actresses, models, and musicians
Why I can't I be just like them
With a hole in my heart
And money to spend
I have to feed the greedy monster within
Ka-Ching!

Deeper and deeper
In debt I go
Why can't this monster just leave me alone?
Ka-Ching!

Credit cards
Bill collectors
And my debts
growing higher and higher still
When will this monster expire?

I plead and beg
Family and friends.
“Save me,” I cry.
Yet there is no reply.
Ka-Ching!

Husband, family, and friends all gone
Lost in a dark world of greed
Consumed by my monster.
Ka-Ching!

The Universal Woman

Nathan and Carolyn are the parents of eight boys and two girls ranging in ages from 2 to 17 years. We had a few friendly encounters with them. After one of these encounters, I learned Carolyn was involved with the children at her church just as I am in my own. We decided to spend a morning together, Christmas and grocery shopping. On a mild December morning we left with her oldest daughter and son for a day out on the town. It was during this time that I began to realize, despite our differences in culture, the bond between two married women knows no boundaries.

To be honest, I was excited about the trip since we decided to go together days before. I liked spending time with Carolyn before. I'm a curious people-person who loves to get to know more about different cultures. I had grown up in an area of Ohio where the Amish were, and still are, prevalent. I know what it means to be the subject of discrimination and public misconception. The Amish face those facets of mainstream America every time they step foot into our consumer-driven world. Yet despite this foreknowledge, I decided to be seen in public with them. When I began this journey I could never know how truly a shopping trip meant more than buying supplies.

At first I was kind of nervous. Carolyn and I had talked about recipes and cultures before. I had no reason to think I'd offend her. Yet like all new relationships, we held onto our comfort zones. She shopped with her two children while I hit the food aisles in Wal-Mart. Moments later; we reconnected in the Christmas aisle. She told me that in her church families exchanged names of children to buy presents for. It reminded me of the white elephant gift exchange I had done in the past. The Amish do that? One of the names on her list was her eighteen-year-old niece who has Down's Syndrome. Her niece loves to play with balls and there was a specific ball she wanted to buy for her. I also learned that instead of buying so many gifts for her children, the school provides for the kids. After all, as she put it to me, the season isn't about getting presents but about Jesus' birth. She and Nathan do buy presents for the two boys who aren't old enough for school. What parent of a two- and four-year-old wouldn't want to make it fair for the younger ones too?

We traveled from store to store sharing our hearts with one another. We had so much fun we lost track of time. We began to understand one another a bit more and found commonalities. Carolyn began to transform from just the Amish wife to a woman before my eyes. I learned details such as Nathan's preference for nuts and honey over refined sugar and her love of cheese products. We smiled and joked around like wives do about husbands. I already knew she spoke three languages. At home they speak Swiss, in church German, and in school they learn English. But what I didn't know was that she reads German.

I introduced her to aspects of my husband's culture, and she was amazed when I brought her to the world foods aisle. I tend to cook more Chinese, Italian, and Hispanic dishes over anything else. It was a new adventure for her. With twelve mouths to feed daily, each with their own distinctive tastes, I could see how introducing a different kind of meal could be problematic. Carolyn has to be wise in her shopping.

As the morning wore into the early afternoon, I gained a greater respect for my Amish neighbor. Wise and resourceful, Carolyn taught me no matter what culture you come from, a woman is still a woman. We have compassionate hearts for our children, a loving devotion to our husbands, and the same emotions. A loving mother, she knows her children's distinctive personalities well. What mother wouldn't? At the end of the day, aren't we all someone's mother, sister, child, and wife? Don't we all have to wear the many hats womanhood brings? Womanhood, a human universal.

Grandma

The thought of death doesn't elude me
As I sit upon the hard, cold ground
Just beside your tombstone
Beckoning my sorrows
I never thought this day would come

Life without you, Grandma
Seems so unbearable
Why did you leave me?
Memories of the joyous days
we shared fill my mind
The past my friend
The future without you, my enemy.
Oh how I will miss your
Laughter, wisdom, and love.

My heart cries with sorrow!
Who will sing to me the songs of long ago?
Who will listen to my stories?
Who will share a strawberry shake with me?
Who will I confide my secrets to?
Now that you are gone?

Grandma, Oh Grandma!
You taught me life-long lessons
And showered me with unconditional love
You laid the foundations of my faith
And taught me to chase my dreams

A world without you
How can I go on?
My guide and friend
Blessed by all who called you their grandmother
You possessed a gentle heart
Kind spirit and unyielding faith
Mourned by many

Yet only a few truly knew you

You, my gracious wise grandmother
Rest with the angels now
Reconnected with those who have gone on before you
Never forgotten and always loved

I shall be the woman you want me to become.
Never forgetting you
or the lessons you have taught me
Grandma, O Grandma
Your time has come.

Before there was Barbie...

There was...

The Gibson Girl

She was the American vision of beauty. Tall and slender with ample bosoms, hips, and bottom, her torso abnormally contoured into an S shape with the help of a swan-bill corset. Her long hair gathered on top of her head in either a pompadour, bouffant, or chignon fashion. Elegantly dressed, she was an independent woman from the upper-class. She was the vision of American beauty and youthfulness. Every American woman wanted to be just like her. Who was this American beauty? The Gibson Girl.

The Gibson girl first appeared in Life magazine on April 9, 1890, just six short years before the Progressive Age began. Although she had been created in the Victorian Age, she would have an everlasting effect on the young women of the Progressive Age. Her creator was Charles Dana Gibson, an illustrator for Life and other magazines. Gibson had wanted to create a different image of Victorian women, one that would show an athletic, sensible, independent woman who was a man's equal and represented the American woman. When questioned how he came about creating the Gibson Girl, Gibson once answered, "I'll tell you how I got what you have called the 'Gibson Girl.' I saw her on the streets, I saw her at the theatres, I saw her in the churches. I saw her everywhere and doing everything. I saw her idling on Fifth Avenue and at work behind the counters of the stores...The nation made the type. What Zangwill calls the 'Melting Pot of Races' has resulted in a certain character; why should it not also have turned out a certain type of face?...There isn't any 'Gibson Girl,' but there are many thousands of American girls, and for that let us all thank God."

Women all over the United States quickly fell in love with his image and wanted more. For more than twenty years, the Gibson Girl appeared not only in magazines and newspapers but her image also graced merchandise such as saucers, ashtrays, tablecloths, pillow covers, chair covers, souvenir spoons, screens, fans, umbrella stands. Middle-class woman idolized the Gibson Girl as she represented the American dream. Men wanted to marry any woman who was just like the Gibson Girl. Out went the Victorian fashions of the day and in came the Gibson Girl fashions. From the top of her head to the tip of her toes, every woman in America mimicked the Gibson Girl. The Gibson Girl reached the height of her popularity in 1900. Twelve years later, at the advent of WWI, she disappeared, never to be forgotten.

Who Were The Models For The Gibson Girls?

Every artist needs a model, and Charles Dana Gibson found her in three different women. One of the earliest models for the Gibson Girl came after the Gibson Girl frenzy had already begun. Irene Langhorn had met Charles Dana Gibson at a dinner in New York City where she had been the guest of honor during the summer of 1894. A year later, he went to her father to ask for her hand in marriage. Her father was not impressed with him and thought the match would not be wise. Irene was a southern belle. She could do better than to marry a "Yankee sign painter." Eventually Charles' charm won Irene's father over. The two were married in Richmond, Virginia on November 7, 1895, at Saint Paul's Episcopal Church. The marriage ceremony was interrupted several times by scholars C. Vann Woodward, Glenda Gilmore, and many others who sought to declare the wedding to be a symbolic marriage between the North and the South. Writer James Fox had declared the marriage was the "symbolic end of the Civil War." Raised as a southern belle, Irene effectively ended that tradition by becoming the independent Gibson Girl!

Another model Gibson used for the Gibson Girl was Evelyn Nesbit. Evelyn had moved to New York City with her mother when she was just sixteen years old. Her mother had been unable to find work, so Evelyn went back into modeling. Evelyn had been a model in Philadelphia but when her mother had moved to New York she did not want her daughter to pursue modeling. Evelyn had used a letter of introduction from an artist in Philadelphia in order to secure a sitting with James Carroll Beckwith. Beckwith was impressed with her and introduced her to several artists. Afterward, Nesbit became one the most demanded models of her time. She was not only sitting for sketches but posed for photographic fashion modeling, where she found the most lucrative jobs. One of the sketches Charles Dana Gibson had done of Nesbit is called The Eternal Question. It was published in 1905 and became one of the most popular of his sketches. The sketch shows the side of Nesbit's face and her red hair drawn in the form of a question mark.

The last model Charles Dana Gibson found inspiration from was the Belgian-born stage actress, Camille Clifford. Although quite beautiful in her own right, it wasn't Camille's facial beauty that had inspired Charles, but her fashion. Camille was known for her hourglass figure and towering hairstyles that were unique for her time. She was known for wearing long gowns that would show off her 18-inch waistline. Gibson was so intrigued by her sense of fashion that he incorporated her fashions into the Gibson Girl. She became the best-known Gibson Girl model.

These three woman may have been the most famously known of the Gibson models, but let's not forget Charles Dana Gibson had claimed to receive his inspiration for the Gibson Girls from his day-to-day encounters with American women.

Like A Mirror

Like a mirror that runs through time,
I see her image so close to mine.
With a name I so adore
She holds the key to my door.
For with this key
This child so sweet
Unlocks the world of evermore.

A world of time is now at my feet
As she sets it free like a balloon floating high in the air
She giggles with glee
As I now understand completely

This child with a life so close to mine
Will be the next in time
To follow my footsteps in every way
Then she said with a heart full of gold,
"I am young but you are old.
For as I grow you will see
How close a pair we will be.
For I am you and you are me.
And we will live eternally"

Mary's Song

I was blessed by a scandal
Pregnant, before marriage
My beloved baby boy,
Born in a manger,
You blessed my life with controversy.

Flesh of my flesh
Son of God
You came into a simple life
Born to a carpenter and his wife.

I watched as you grew
In Egypt and Galilee
More children came yet it always remained,
You were my favorite son
My first-born son!

The day your father died
You were a man
I smiled and I cried
No longer my boy
But the man of our household.

I never knew
But I guess I should have
How great a man
You would become

On that day
When you went away
I wondered
Will he be okay out on his own?

What magnificent deeds
I heard you did
You cured the sick
And healed so many

You preached hope, love, and peace
My baby born
A mother could not be more proud to call you her son

And to me it ended that day
The day they took you away
I anguished as you were beaten, bruised
And taken to the cross.

He's innocent!
My baby boy is innocent!
I cried inside
What injustice
I did not understand
How could a mother do so
When her baby boy is willing to be nailed to the cross?

I cried.
I anguished.
I saw you die!
My manger baby
God's own son
Gone!

But glory be
I saw the tomb
Three days later
Your body was gone!

You came to me
And the others
Speaking words of hope
My manger baby
Now my savior and king
Glory be!

What is a Quaker?

During the 17th century, Europe experienced a turbulent time of religious persecutions. Catholic and Protestant Churches maintained political power of their given country. Those who did not conform to the mainstream church were considered heretics, arrested, tortured and eventually killed. Both the Protestants and Catholic churches maintained there was only one true faith. In order to preserve the uniformity of the faith, dissenters must be punished without mercy. For example, in 1630, one Puritan lay person had been found guilty of heresy and had been given the following punishment: life imprisonment, his property confiscated, his nose slit, an ear cut off, and his forehead branded "S.S." (sower of sedition). To evade religious persecution, different groups such as the Quakers soon migrated to American colonies where they could worship peacefully and begin better lives for themselves.

The Quaker movement had been founded in 1652 by George Fox of England. Like, Martin Luther, he never sought to start a religious movement, yet as he preached he began to gather a following. George's ideas at the time were radical. He believed:

- Rituals can be safely ignored, as long as one experiences a true spiritual conversion.
- The qualification for ministry is given by the Holy Spirit , not by ecclesiastical study. This implies that anyone has the right to minister, assuming the Spirit guides them, including women and children.
- God "dwelleth in the hearts of his obedient people": religious experience is not confined to a church building; indeed, Fox refused to apply the word "church" to a building, using instead the name "steeple-house", a usage maintained by many Quakers today. Fox would just as soon worship in fields and orchards, believing that God's presence could be felt anywhere.
- Though Fox used the Bible to support his views, Fox reasoned that, because God was within the faithful, believers could follow their own inner guide rather than

rely on a strict reading of Scripture or the word of clerics

- As the Bible makes no mention of the Trinity, Fox also made no clear distinction between Father, Son and Holy Spirit. (wikipedia)

Quakers were pacifists, which meant they would not fight in any of the king's wars nor would they pay taxes if they believed the money was to aide in the military. They also believed in total equality. A Quaker would never bow down to a noble, because they were equals. The belief in total equality also meant Quaker women found greater freedom than their Orthodox Christian counterparts. Women were allowed to preach, take part in politics, and speak in their meetings. To the nobles, a Quaker could never be trusted since Quakers did not believe in taking oaths.

The Orthodox Church in England viewed the Quakers as a threat to the uniformity of the true faith and began to persecute them. During the 1650's a thousand Quakers were held in English prisons. During this time, George Fox's view of traditional and social practices within the church had become hardened. He outlawed water baptism, stating a person's conversion should be evident through an inner change and not marked by baptism. During this time, the Quakers grew in population and began to hold larger meetings. They also travelled to the different prisons where the other Quakers had been held in order to get the testimony of their sufferings. The various stories would be gathered then presented once a year at the Meeting for Sufferings.

Twenty years later, the Quakers were still being persecuted in England while some of their members had begun a new life for themselves in New Jersey. According to the website Religion and Founding of America, "by 1680, 10,000 Quakers had been imprisoned in England, and 243 had died of torture and mistreatment in the King's jails." In 1681, William Penn, gave his fellow Quakers an opportunity of a lifetime. Leave England for a land of religious freedoms and no tax-supported churches. Four years later, there were as many as 8,000 Quakers in Pennsylvania. A quarter of the heads of households had been in English prisons.

The Voice

Late at night
I hear him calling my name
His sweet voice
Gently stirs me from my deep slumber

I wonder
Oh how I wonder
Was it just a dream
Or had my Lord spoken to me?

Did I not hear the sound of a child's laughter?
Was his voice not in the delicate breeze
Blowing through my open window?
How many nights has he called my name,
Yet still I do not answer.

My heart stirs with regret
How can I run and hide from him?
He who knows and sees all.
God.
The very word brings reverence upon my lips.
"I'm here," I cry.

Seeing is Believing

Seeing is believing
So people say
Seeing is believing
Takes my faith away

When seeing is believing
My heart grows cold
How can I trust a savior
Who died so long ago?

Seeing is believing
Even Thomas claimed
Yet when Thomas saw his Lord's wounds
He was changed that very day.

Seeing is not believing
For the eyes can lie
My human mind twists the truth
I see what I want to see

For the truth lies in the heart
If seeing is believing, then let my actions reveal
God lives within my heart

A Caring Father

Boundless love
Joyfully caring
He is always there for me

Why, oh why, did I try to hide?
Am I not where I'm supposed to be?

Forgive me, father
My loving father,
For I am not as happy as I should be.
I was foolish and arrogant to disobey.
Yet now I know you did not discipline me out of spite.
For you father,
Care for me.

The Manger

Once upon a manger,
Laid my savior
He was born of a virgin
And raised as a carpenter

Once upon a river,
my savior
Baptized by John
But blessed by God

Once upon a cross
Hung my savior
Strong yet sore,
He cried, "No more."

Now upon heaven
Sits my savior
Saying to me
"Come, be with me."

You were on his mind

In the darkness of nothingness
Before the world began
You were on his mind.

After creation
It was not the beauty of the world
The plants nor animals
It was you on his mind.

Our father, Abraham
Was told of God's plan
"Look to the sky.
See all those stars…"
You were on God's mind.

My lord, my lord
The day Jesus was born
You were on his mind.

He has felt our pain
He has known fear
He lived this life
Cause you were on his mind.

On that fateful day,
Jesus was crucified
God turned his back on his son
and wept a tear
Full of all our sins,
He couldn't be near him
He'd rather see his own son die
Than to lose you
You were on his mind

Precious Princess,
Daughter of God
Valiant Prince,
Son of God
You are so loved in His mind
The most cherished creation has ever made
You are always on HIS mind.

Candlelight

Candlelight,
candlelight
Oh, what a sight

Red of passion
Orange of desire
Yellow for the heart of gold

Candlelight
Candlelight
Oh, what a sight

He has given me love
He has given me life
No longer alone
His fire burns bright

Candlelight
Candlelight
Oh, what a sight!

The Garden

I am a garden of life
I have survived the rainstorms of destruction and pain
I have bloomed on those bright summer days.

My garden of weeds
called worries and woes
Next to the flowers
of hopes and dreams

I've planted self-centeredness
Next to unselfishness
And my anger grows close to glee

The master gardener
Plucks my weeds of destruction and dismay
He replants them with flowers of grace, love, and mercy
Once barren trees now
overflowing
The fruits of the spirit.

Seasons come
And seasons go
But one thing always remains
My master gardener lovingly cares for this garden
Pruning, weeding, and transplanting
Until His work is done
And all that remains
Is a reflection of the Son.

Hope

Knowing he's there
Every night
Every day
Praying for the end to draw near

Peace will be won when the
Righteous fight
After the dark
Yearning with anticipation I await the
Important day when
Right has won and
Gone is the evil one

Never again will
Evil be near
Victorious will be our song
Every angel will sing
Righteousness has won

God gave us the power
Intelligence and strength
Very important gifts with
Everlasting unconditional love

Up in heaven the
Prince has won

Nightlight

Night-light
Night bright
Illuminating darkness
Darkness surrounds me
But I dare not hide
From the fears that abide in me

My body no longer
Tossing and turning
Saved by the nightlight in me
My little nightlight I adore

This tiny nightlight deep within
Stands proud and strong
Calling, O calling me
Trust me, the voice says

Demons and monsters live in the night
They dare not come near me
O what a sight!
My little nightlight
Shines so bright
Illuminating the path before me
Casting my fears aside

The Final Journey

The bright light guides me through the tunnel
that connects this world to the next.
Oh what a sight I see before me!
Family, friends, and childhood heroes who passed before me
Greet me at Heaven's door.

No longer do I feel the aches and pains of my body.
Happiness and joy fill my heart.
Those dear to my heart greet me
with a warm embrace.
Then suddenly my Lord appears.
"Well done faithful servant.
Welcome home," He speaks to me.

Oh, how His words spill from His mouth
like honey to my ears.
Glorious and righteous,
behold His illuminating beauty.
Nothing can compare.

Speechless and humbled by His magnificent presence
I feel His unconditional love.
"Follow me," He instructs.
I follow Him through the golden streets
with my friends and family behind me.
Angels sing their glorious song,
"Another child returns to the Father through the Son.
Halleluiah, she gave him her all."

In front of the judgment throne my savior stands in front of me.
Radiant and omnipresent,
God sits upon His towering throne.
Satan recalls the many sins of my life,
Prosecuting me to the almighty judge.
With arms open wide Jesus proclaims,
"She is your child, heavenly Father.

She gave her life on earth to me.
She's without sin. I bore it all."

The final judgment.
My heart skips with fear.
I always knew this day would come.
God stares into my face and declares,
"I see no sin. She's white as snow.
Go away from here, Satan.
She's my daughter."
With a wave of his hand,
that fallen angel disappears.

Sunset

Dripping colors
of blue, purple, yellow, and orange
escape from God's paintbrush

Back and forth
He strokes his brush
Granting his beloved children
another unique masterpiece of color.

Every day, the sky above me tells a new story
Never the same.
How I long to see
what he has created for his children today.
I am in wonder and awe at the Master Artist.
Oh, what creativity!
Oh what splendors he creates!

With a sky that seems to go on forever,
His canvas so wide
He does not disappoint.
Peace and serenity envelop me.
As I wait and watch his beautiful painting.

Just A Little Farther

It's just a little farther
Nothing there or here
Just a little farther
Do I even dare?

So many days,
So many years
I should have gone just a little farther
Instead I remained
Wondering and waiting
Yet just a little farther
My answer was near

Just a little farther
Was a man who needed my help
Just a little farther
Was a boy who loved me
Just a little farther
My dream job awaited me

When will I ever learn
That just a little farther
Lies my hope?

Sunflowers and Cactus

Sunflowers bless the land in my loving father's holy name
Under the sun it raises its head high to the heavens with a cry
No more shall evil take this land let not
Fear dwell in the hearts of man only
Love abounds this earth they grow upon
Only the sunflower honors the grass under my feet
Waiting for my savior to appear
Ever so happy they lift their heads in anticipation of his return
Ready to signal his glorious return
Signaling with their head turned towards the sun, He is the only one

As the Native Americans cherish dear
No evil dwells upon the land where the sunflower grows
Daily they remind us keep your eyes on God.

Caution dwells in the human heart, well away from the fertile grass
Alone the cactus dwells within the harsh desert.
Courage it takes to survive in such a place
Thorns protecting it from hate, evil, and destruction
Under the rigors of life it cries to God
Save me, Savior, deliver me from my heartache.

Inside The Man Who Started It All: George Washington

George Washington was born February 22, 1732 on Pope Creek's Estate near Westmoreland, Virginia Colony. His parents were Augustine and Mary Ball Washington. George was the third generation to be born in the colonies. Before immigrating to the colonies, the Washington family had held prominence in England. During the Puritan Revolt of the 1640's (aka The English Civil War), the family lost a majority of their wealth. In 1657, King Henry VIII granted Lawrence Washington 5,000 acres in the Virgina Colony. George's great grandfather immigrated to Virginia. Not much is known about George's father's side of the family in the colonies until Augustine's birth.

Augustine Washington's father had died when Augustine was only four years old. After his father's death, he and his sister split the inheritance. Augustine gained 1,000 acres and slaves on Bridges Creek in Westmoreland County. Soon after he gained his inheritance he married his first wife, Jane Butler. Jane was an orphan and through their marriage he gained approximately 640 more acres that she had inherited through her father. Augustine and Jane had four children together. A year after they were married, Jane gave birth to a son, Butler, who died before the age of one. Augustine not only built a family but also increased the couple's land holdings. Augustine was an ambitious man. He built mills, grew tobacco, acquired land, and owned slaves. At one time he had even tried his hand in opening up iron mines. In 1726, Augustine had a new home for his wife and children built, called Wakefield. That same year, he also bought his sister's land and slaves. When he wasn't working on his land he was very active in the Anglican Church. He also served as a Justice of the Peace and a sheriff. On November 24, 1729, Jane died unexpectedly, leaving Augustine to raise their children Lawrence (age 11), Augustine (age 9), and Jane (age 7) by himself. Two years later, he remarried, this time to

23-year-old Mary Ball of Lancaster County. Mary gave birth to their first child, George Washington. The couple would have five more children: Elizabeth Washington (1733-1797), Samuel Washington (1734-1781), John Augustine Washington (1736-1787), Charles Washington (1738-1799), and Mildred Washington (1739-1740). Tragedy hit Augustine during times of joy. Four years into his marriage, as Mary continued to give him children, Jane died. After the death of Jane, Augustine moved his family up the Potomac River to the Little Hunting Creek Plantation (aka Mount Vernon). The family would remain there until 1738, whereupon Augustine moved his family to Ferry Farm on the Rappahannock River, close to Fredericksburg. Here George Washington spent much of his youth.

Although a member of gentile population, George's family was never considered upper class. His family was considered to be a member of the middling class, since they were only moderately wealthy. As a boy, George was homeschooled from ages 7 to 15 by the local church sexton and later by a schoolmaster. George excelled in mathematics. He was taught all morals, manners, and educations that were expected of a man of his station. His educations included geography, mathematics, Latin, and Classical English. Although he had a wonderful education, it would be the knowledge he gained from the planation foreman and backwoodsmen that he would utilize for most of his life. By the time he had finished his educations, George had become a master tobacco farmer, surveyor, and stock raiser.

Not much is known about George Washington's childhood except for the fables, such as how he chopped down his father's favorite cherry tree. George's father died of stomach gout on April 12, 1743. At the time of Augustine's death he had several plantations with a total of 64 slaves assigned throughout. In Augustine’s will, Lawrence had been given guardianship of George. Lawrence made certain George had an excellent up-bringing. Lawrence had also been given the estate at Little Hunting Creek Planation, along with the slaves. Lawrence soon renamed the planation Mount Vernon in honor of Admiral Edward Vernon of the British Navy.

George stayed with his mother and helped her run the plantation until he was 16, when he decided to travel with a surveying group. A year later, Lawrence's father-in-law, Lord Fairfax, appointed George as the official surveyor of Culpeper County. Two years later, as Lawrence suffered from tuberculosis, George traveled to Barbados with his brother in hopes that the tropical weather would cure his brother. At the same time, George was suffering from smallpox. George's survival of the smallpox was vital for his future, in that it inoculated him from the terrible disease that would later kill most of his troops in the Revolutionary War. The disease had left his face slightly scarred. The trip to Barbados had proved futile for his brother. Lawrence died at Mount Vernon in July of 1752. Lawrence and his wife had four children, only one of whom survived; a two-year-old daughter named Sarah. Two months after her father's death, Sarah died, leaving George to inherit Mount Vernon at 20 years of age.

Marion, Ohio's Own: President Warren G. Harding

My mother's family came to this county before the United States existed. My ancestors fought in the Revolutionary War. After the war ended we travelled into the Ohio Wilderness where my family settled into the Ohio Territory. We were there when Ohio became a state. We were there to help form Marion County, Ohio and we were there when Marion, Ohio became a town. My family has seen Marion, Ohio grown from a small town into the small city it is today. We have seen Presidents come and go from President Washington to President Obama but none have lived closer them than President Warren G. Harding.

Warren G. Harding was born the eldest of eight children, on November 2, 1865 in Marion, Ohio to Dr. George Tyron Harding, Sr. and Phoebe Elizabeth (Dickerson) Harding. At the age of 10, Warren began to work with his father on the small family owned and operated local newspaper, *The Argus.* There he fell in love with the newspaper trade. Harding attended the Ohio Central College in Iberia, Ohio where he studied printing and newspaper trade. In 1882, at 16 years of age, he graduated with a Bachelor of Science. He was an accomplished public speaker. Four years later, he bought the Marion Daily Star, one of three newspapers in the city for $300. The strongest read paper at the time was *The Marion Independent*. Harding worked hard to unset the paper and move his own into its position. The effort took its toll on Harding. In 1889, he suffered from exhausted and nervous fatigue but his paper was one of the most popular newspapers of Marion County. After spending several weeks at the Battle Creek Sanitarium, Harding returned to his beloved paper. In 1891, Harding married Florence Kling DeWolfe, the daughter of his newspaper nemesis, Amos Hall King. By 1896, *the Marion Daily Star* became so popular his rival newspapers had gone out of business. It became so strong; Harding and his wife were able to travel around the country, which exposed Harding at political gatherings.

The following years, Harding moved out of the newspaper business and into politics. In 1889, he served two terms on Ohio State

Senate for the 13th Senatorial District then was awarded the Lt. Governorship of Ohio from 1904 to 1906. In 1910 he ran for Ohio State Governor but lost the race to the incumbent Judson Harmon. During his presidential campaign of 1920, Harding held many speeches from railcars and his front porch. Many came from all over to hear him. He won the election and served as U.S. President from 1921-1923. President Warren G. Harding died in mid conversation with his wife at 7:35pm on August 2, 1923 from a heart attack. President Harding was buried in Marion, Ohio on August 10, 1923. His wife died on November 21, 1924. On December 20, 1927 both the President and his wife's bodies were reburied at the new Harding Memorial. You can visit both their graves today and their house.

A Writer's Recipe

A pinch of inspiration
A heaping of encouraging friends
A touch of writing groups
A dash of your own blood, sweat, and tears
1 teaspoon endurance
1 teaspoon perseverance
2 cups of imaginary friends who talk to you
1 cup of captivating plot lines
1/4 cup of beta readers
1/4 cup of editors
1/4 cup of reviewers

Mix together inspiration, encouraging friends, and writing groups until you have a pleasant, creamy liquid mixture. Set aside until needed. Stir your blood, sweat, and tears with perseverance, endurance, your imaginary friends, and plot lines until smooth. Periodically add a tablespoon of the creamy mixture you had set aside to ensure your batter is light and smooth. Do this several times through the process until your batter is consistent and breathes with the aroma of freshness. If there is reserve left over do not throw it away, but set it aside for another day. Bake it in the oven at 350 degrees until it is refined. Take it out and let it cool while you make the frosting. Mix together the beta readers, editors, and reviewers until you have a frosting that is creamy and delicious! Place the frosting on top of the writer's "cake." It only makes the "cake" taste better. Enjoy!

The Bookworm

Wonder by wonder
I travel to places I've never been
Dazzling places I've never known
Time under my control

Daring princes
Monsters to slay
A murder to solve
A game to play

Far off places
Adventure, romance, suspense, O my
Characters so real
I cry when they die!

Up and down my emotions run.
I can't read but just one!
More, give me, I cry
I must have more!

Hardback, paperback, kindle
I don't care
Just give me something to read
If you dare.

Amazon, library, and bookstores alike
Feed my addiction
Book by book
They are my delight!
Who needs television, film, or radio
When a book can give you so much more

Page by page
My world disappears
Until I forget my own.

Glorious, wonderful books!
I can't have but one.
How would I survive?

The Mind and the Laptop

Portable library of immense information,
learning and organizing data from within.
Speed is my friend.
Processing and calculating,
my intellectual thoughts cease when I die.

Never a day goes by,
something new doesn't intrigue me.
Researching and learning,
together my laptop and I manipulate data.

Tiny pockets of organized facts,
sit within my brain and upon my laptop's wall.
Streams of memories,
photographic images of my life,
word documents, video, and tiny useless facts,
all stored away in my mental and computerized library.

The information highway beckons me.
Travel, explore, meet new people and do more things.
My mind controls portions of my body,
as the CPU controls my laptop's internal system.

How alike my supercomputer brain is to my laptop.
Yet how different we can be.
One alive and the other an inanimate object,
Two minds controlling applications and systems.
My laptop and me.

The Native Muse

She watches earnestly with wisdom,
this Native American woman on my desktop wallpaper.
Guarding my writings and photography,
she beckons the writer within me.

I heed her call.
What wonders will she take me to today?
Shall we ride the plains with the Blackfeet or Sioux?
Or dance with the Shawnee around the great campfire?
Follow the Navajo sheepherders?
Or fish with the great Pacific tribes?

Words spread across my Microsoft Word.
Images of lands far away,
people, creatures, and ideas
foreign to my fast-paced, computerized world
Yet familiar to her.

A moment becomes a day.
Lost in time, I forget the keys under my fingers.
Paragraphs become reality.
I lose myself in the plot.
Suspense, history, romance, and danger await me.

Her world transforms my thoughts.
No longer am I the writer,
I actively take part in her story.
Her ideas and speech create emotions I'd never felt before.

The land, the people, and the ideas - they're so real.
Her story becomes my own.
I want to press on.
I have to know more.
She guides me through her story
only to release me into my own reality.

I lean back from my computer,
released from my creative endeavor.
My Native American muse sits quietly
upon my desktop wallpaper,
with a stare towards me.
Her secret journey my own,
given to those who dare to read.

The Path

Winding rivers of trails
Unseen to the white man's eyes
I follow our people down the hillside.

Twisting, turning, confusing the white man
Paths twist and turn like a giant spider web
Follow them all they lead to nowhere

Follow the rivers and creeks
The other tribes tell us
The water shall quench your thirst on your long journey.

We dare not to tread where others have led
The white man shouldn't be able to find
What the vast forest hides.

Who Are The Shawnee?

I Am Shawnee!

Shawnee. The very word unifies them as a nation. Yet in all of Shawnee history, the only time they ever came together as one people was when there was a threat against all Shawnee people. The Shawnee have always lived an independent lifestyle. To be an adult Shawnee meant you could live wherever you wanted without the need to answer to anyone. This allowed the Shawnee the freedom to settle anywhere which is why when the settlers began to explore the wilderness it was very easy for them to run into a Shawnee.

One of the problems the Europeans faced with the Shawnee people was the idea of political unity. The Europeans' concept of leadership was completely different than the Shawnee. They were coming for a culture where monarchy was the rule of the land. This meant everyone obeyed one leader. To the Shawnee this was a foreign concept. While they did have chiefs, they could leave the chief's leadership if they disagreed with the chief. So when a chief makes an agreement with another he is speaking for his village but if a person does not agree with the comprise he or she is free to leave without any political repercussions. The Europeans had expected if a compromise was made with a Shawnee chief then it was to be followed by all Shawnee. In the Shawnee's eyes, the compromise was made only with his or her village not the entire nation. The cultural differences in this belief often mistakenly lead the Europeans in conflict with the Shawnee.

Shawnee Leadership

The Shawnee people lived a life that revolved around their conservative religious beliefs. They believed their creator, Our Grandmother, created five divisions of their people. These five divisions were: *Chillicothe* (Chalahgawtha) [Chalaka, Chalakatha], *Hathawekela* (Asswikales, Sweickleys, etc.) [Thawikila], *Kispokotha* (Kispoko) [kishpoko, kishpokotha], *Mequachake* (Mekoche, Machachee, Maguck, Mackachack) [Mekoche] and *Pekuwe* (Piqua, Pekowi, Pickaway, Picks) [Pekowi, Pekowitha]. Each division had their own set of responsibilities.

We shall go into this further in another posting. For now, let us focus on the Chillicothe and the Kishpoko.

Ideally the leadership of a village was lead under two chiefs. All villages had a council of elders that were like advisers to the chief. No chief could make a decision without seeking the advice of the elders. Council meetings were often held for three days. The two chiefs were the peace chief and the war chief. The two did not come from the same division nor did they lead their people at the same time.

The peace chief came from the Chillicothe division. He was responsible for leading the village in times of peace and only answered to the principal peace chief. The principal peace chief was the peace leader over of all the Shawnee. Each summer the village peace chiefs would travel to the principal peace chief's village for a great council. The position of peace chief was hereditary. It could only be passed from father to son. The principal chief was chosen from the independent village chiefs. A famous Shawnee peace chief was Chief Cornstalk. The peace chief's wife was known as the female peace chief. She had the responsibility of overseeing the female duties of the village, ordering when to plant and sow the fields and scheduled the cooking for the feasts. Women had a strong voice in the tribal government because the Shawnee honored women more than men.

One of the most well-known war chiefs was Tecumseh.

The position of war chief was not hereditary. After the war chief died any Kishpoko could compete for the position. The competitors were given men underneath their leadership for the duration of three seperate village attacks. They had to prove themselves by gathering a scalp from each attack and arrive home without any of their warriors killed or injured. Than the man who could do this three times was said to be chosen by Our Grandmother to replace the war chief. A war chief could only come out of the Kishpoko division since these were the warriors of the Shawnee nation. Tecumseh's father was the principal war chief until his death when Tecumseh was still a boy. Tecumseh was too young at that time to fight for his father's position.

The war chief led the village during the times of war. He was also responsible for training all boys to become warriors and strong providers. Whenever the village was at war it would be the war chief who was in charge and not the peace chief. You could always tell the distinction between the chiefs because a war chief always wore a red tipped tomahawk on his hip. The war chief, like the peace chief, also answered to a principal chief and travelled in the summer to the a great council. Another responsibility of the war chief was to ensure law and order in the village. He was the emissary sent to other tribes to speak on behalf of his village. So more often, the Europeans, when they were encountering a village leader it was not the peace chief they were speaking too but the war chief. The war chief would not make a decision without consulting the peace chief first. This is why they rarely made a decision when speaking to the Europeans about anything. They would have to take the information back to the village, discuss it with the peace chief and council then deliver the decision to the tribe or Europeans. The Europeans did not understand this and often grew impatient waiting for their reply.

Like the peace chief, the war chief's wife also served beside her husband in the leadership of their people. Known as the war woman, she was responsible for examining the captives. If her husband was about to attack a village or kill a captive and she disapproved she could speak up against it. He could not act without her consent if she decided to protect them.

Shawnee Origins

The Shawnee were a Central Algonquian speaking people. Linguistically, this means they were related to the Sauk-Fox-Kickapoo, Miami-Illinois, Ojibwe-Potawatomi, Menominee, and the Cree-Montagnais-Naskapi. The name Shawnee comes from the Algonquian word, Shawunogi, which means "Southerners." The Shawnee prefer to call themselves Shawano. The Shawnee were very conservative people. They believed they must obey a strict set of laws, known as creeds, that Our Grandmother had handed down to them in order to learn how to live a faithful life. Some of their customs and beliefs set them apart from their neighboring tribes.

The Shawnee creation story is very unique for the Algonquian group in that the Shawnee are the only tribe to believe they had crossed open waters at the time of creation. Also unique to them is the belief that a female deity, known as Our Grandmother, had created everything. The Shawnee believed in a supreme being known as Moneto, aka Great Spirit, who had the idea for creation. According to the Shawnee story, "In the beginning there was the Great Spirit, formed of wind, invisible, but in the shape of a man. He lived above the sun. There was just space; no earth, no water. The Great Spirit said, 'Let there be woman' and as soon as he spoke there was a being formed as a woman. Then to this woman the Great Spirit gave the work of creating this earth, light (the sun), water, people, and animals. She is the one the people saw and knew. Before the flood she and the devil and her grandson and the great giants were all on this earth which she made, and the people talked to them. In this first creation, people lived a long time and died four times, but not so today. The Great Spirit must have made the sky, or again it might mean that the Great Spirit was the sky. The female creator (Our Grandmother) is under the Great Spirit. Afterward the female creator did her creating and made the rules which are to be fulfilled."

According to George Bluejacket at Wapaughkonnetta on October 29, 1829 this is how the Shawnee had survived the great flood:

"The beginning of the Shawanoe tribe was when the Go-cum-tha (our grandmother) of our people come up out of the great salt water holding to the tail of the Ne-she-pe-she (Panther).

Her Wash-et-che (Husband) was carried to the shore by a very big Wa-be-the (Swan or Goose). The land where their people had lived was swallowed up in the great salt water by Watch-e-men-e-toc (Bad Spirit or Devil), but Mish-e-me-ne-toc (The Great Spirit) saved these two and they were the first of our tribe. Many animals and birds were saved too, so there was plenty of hunting in the new Me-to-quegh-ke (Forest). This was many Te-pe-wa-ko-te (Hundred seasons or years) ago, and our people soon became many. They have always been called Shawanoes (Water people), and the Me-she-pe-she (Panther) and Wa-be-the (Swan) have always been the signs (Emblem or Totem) of this tribe."

Thirty years later, Charles Bluejacket, explained how both the white man and the red man were saved during Noah's flood. He said the white man and his family were in the great canoe that saved the white family, just as the Bible records. As stated above, a red woman had been saved as well. After the flood, Moneto placed her in a valley with a hill between her and her white brother and his family. She could see the smoke from the white man's wigwam. Feeling quite lonely she wept. The Great Spirit came down. She told him she was just an old woman and she was the last of her people. He reminded her of how the first man had been created. After the Great Spirit had left her she began to form children out of clay. She tried to breathe life onto them but nothing worked. She wept. The Great Spirit once again visited her. She told them what had transpired. He once again reminded her of the story of the first men. After the Great Spirit left she breathed into the nostrils of her clay children and they became alive. This was the beginning of the red man. The people were one tribe and grew numerous.

The belief that all red men descended from one woman and were once a part of a great tribe influenced how the Shawnee related to their neighboring tribes. The Shawnee had a special bond with two tribes, the Delaware and the Kickapoo.

The Shawnee and Delaware (Lenni Lenape)

Called the grandfathers by the Shawnee people, the Delaware (known as the Lenni Lenape) shared a close bond with the Shawnee. The Shawnee showed this group of people the utmost respect because they believed the Delaware had been the first tribe to be created after the flood.

"Curiously enough, Our Grandmother did not create the Shawnee first, but they began with the Delaware. When she completed a Delaware man and woman, she put them on the east side of a fire which she had kindled. Then she created one Shawnee division, in the form of an old man and an old woman. After this she created a young man and young woman who were expected to have children who would constitute three of the Shawnee divisions. Here, apparently her interest in creating people ceased...."(Told by Mary Williams, an absentee Shawnee in the book Shawnee by James H. Howard)

Like the tale of the "Roasted Bear Feet" between the Kickapoo and the Shawnee, there is a story that was once told by the Shawnee and Delaware in Pennsylvania of how the Shawnee and Delaware were once one people. The story was lost to both tribes but had been recorded by a white person in the time it was told to him by the tribes. The story is known as "The Grasshopper War." The story is still told today at Native American PowWows. It goes like this:

Deep in the Pennsylvania wilderness, before any white man ever set foot on the land, were two villages. The inhabitants of each village liked to visit one another. The men would hunt together and the women would share their work. Each village enjoyed the company of the other. One day while a boy was visiting he found a grasshopper near a river. He played with his little friend until a group of children came upon them. He showed the grasshopper to his friends and they were all happy playing with the insect together. But one of the boys wasn't happy with the visiting boy's discovery. He thought to himself, "Shouldn't the grasshopper be mine instead of his. This is my village after all." So the upset boy snatched the grasshopper from the visiting boy and ran away with the insect. The children and the boy gave chase. They soon caught up to the thief and the children began to fight, each siding with the boy of their own village. Now the women heard the fight and came out to see what the argument was about. Seeing the blood and bruises of their children they joined in the fight to defend their child and village. The screams grew in the air. Later that day, the men had returned from hunting when they found the females of their family and their children huddled on the ground injured and bloody. The chiefs of both villages wanted vengeance. They declared war upon each other and the men joined their wives and children in battle. After the battle was over, everyone was repulsed by what they had done. A simple argument between boys had led to a battle between friends. Quilt filled their hearts. They decided in order to keep the peace it was best if the two villages went their separate ways. Thus began the Shawnee and Delaware.

The Delaware originally lived along the Northeast Coast of the Atlantic between the Hudson and Delaware rivers. They were one of the first tribes to come into contact with the white man in the early 1600's. A loose confederacy of clans, the largest villages at the time of contact had a population of two to three hundred people. Most of the villages, though, only consisted of 25-30 people. Like Shawnee divisions, the Delaware had three major groups. These were Unalachtigo (Turkey) Unami (Turtle) and Munsee (Wolf). Each group spoke their own dialect.

Like the Shawnee, the Delaware also has a clan system. Unlike the Shawnee, the Delaware were matriarchal. A child would inherit their clan identity from their mother. Hereditary leadership passed down from mother to child. If the women elders did not approve of any leader they could remove that leader from their office. The women controlled agricultural lands but the Delaware did not recognize ownership of the land. Land was collectively owned by whichever clan occupied that area. Unlike the Shawnee, the Delaware did not travel with the season from village to village.

Whenever a young woman married, the couple would reside with her family so her mother and sisters could help with the family. After she gave birth, the most important person in a child's life was his or her mother's eldest brother. The mother's brother would become the child's mentor and would be from a different clan.

The Shawnee and Delaware enjoyed a friendship from long ago. While the Shawnee were in Pennsylvania, they were closely associated with one another. Like the Shawnee, the Delaware were affected by the outbreak of Smallpox during the 17th century. After the Shawnee left Pennsylvania for Ohio, the Delaware stayed behind briefly. Conflicts with the Europeans and the Iroquois contributed to the Delaware abandoning their homelands. In 1766, through a peace treaty with the British, the Delaware moved west across the Allegheny Mountains into Ohio using Shawnee trails. This pattern would continue until the Delaware were removed by the United States to Oklahoma in the 1860's. The Shawnee would always move first, establish the trails then the Delaware would follow.

The two tribes often joined forces to fight a common enemy together. In 1776, the combined forces of Shawnee and Delaware forced the Cherokee to move deeper into the south. The Shawnee and Delaware fought together in the French and Indian War but not the American Revolutionary War. While the Shawnee were helping the British fight against the newly formed American army, the Delaware were one of the first tribes to sign a peace treaty with the leaders of the future United States. In the treaty, the Delaware promised they would aide the patriots by providing food and supplies. The future United States agreed to grant them a place of importance at the head of the new country in return. Although they fought on opposing sides, the Shawnee and Delaware never lost the close relationship. Even today, the Shawnee honor the Delaware.

The Shawnee and the Kickapoo

Although the Delaware and Shawnee people shared a closed relationship, it is with the Kickapoo they resemble more closely in culture and language. Both the Kickapoo and Shawnee people assert that they are related. This comes from a shared myth describing how the Kickapoo and Shawnee had split from a larger tribe. The story is known as "Roasted Bear Feet".

The Shawnee used to be a part of the Kickapoo Nation. One day ten hunters went bear hunting together. They had killed the bear, taken it back to their camp and decided to celebrate their victory by roasting and eating the bear's feet. So the men placed the feet to roast. As the feet were roasting all the men fell asleep. Later three of the men awoke very hungry. They decided, instead of waking their comrades up, they would eat some of the meat. After they ate some of the meat, their friends awoke from their sleep only to find the hind legs had remained. The seven hunters were very upset. They drove the three hunters who had eaten the meat away telling them to get their families and leave them forever. The three hunters and their families became the Kickapoo.

When most people hear the tribe Kickapoo they often think of Texas, Oklahoma, Kansas and Northern Mexico. The Kickapoo are not native to those lands but moved to those areas during the mid - nineteenth century. The descendants of the Kickapoo are scattered throughout regions I mentioned above. Their ancestors were members of a larger tribe that once inhabited the Great Lakes region. The French first encounter the Kickapoo in the early 1640's between Lake Michigan and Lake Erie. There is strong archaeological evidence to support that the Shawnee occupied the same area as the Kickapoo, Delaware and other groups along the Great Lakes region during the first French contact. When the Kickapoo had encountered the French, like the Shawnee, they were very independent and self-sufficient. At the time of contact the Kickapoo were members of a confederacy of tribes known as the Wabash Confederacy. Like the Shawnee's conservatism that sets them apart from other tribes, the Kickapoo also had an attitude that set them apart. They were self-reliant. It is a characteristic that continues even to this day. And like the Shawnee, they established trade relations with the French. The Shawnee did not remain by the Great Lakes for long and moved southward.

The Kickapoo lived a transitory lifestyle that mirrored the lifestyle of the Shawnee. Both groups would move from village to village according to the seasons. The lifestyle suited the Kickapoo well.

By the 1660's the Beaver War with the Iroquois had driven the Kickapoo away from their ancestral homelands into Wisconsin. In Wisconsin they formed a loosely based alliance with other displaced Algonquians. Some of these may have been Shawnee. The Kickapoo had always enjoyed a close alliance with the Shawnee. The Kickapoo participated with the Shawnee and other Algonquian groups in Pontiac's Rebellion. They played a large role in aiding Tecumseh during the War of 1812. Their participation in these efforts not only affected their relationship with the white man but also splintered their own tribe. By the mid-19th century there were three distinct groups of Kickapoo, each living in different areas. These were the Oklahoma Kickapoo, Mexican or Texas Kickapoo and the Kansas Kickapoo. Not much is known about the Kickapoo. The Shawnee have always kept a close alliance with the tribe. In 1900, when the Shawnee chief Big Jim had led some of the Absentee warriors to scout for land in Mexico they had encounter an epidemic of smallpox. The Mexican Kickapoos offered to aid the Shawnee but Chief Big Jim decided he would return with his men to Oklahoma. After he left, the Mexican authorities quarantined the

Shawnee party. Big Jim and all but two of his men died from the disease in September of 1900.

One of the cultural aspects that the Shawnee share with the Kickapoo is a society known as "Miseekwaaweekwaakee." Unlike most Algonquin groups the Shawnee did not employ societies (secret men's clubs) into their organization. But there is one society that did exist. The Man Eaters. The Man Eaters were also found in the Kickapoo culture. The Man Eaters were a military society, yet unlike any other military society, membership was inherited and four women led the group. The Man Eaters would get rid of the body of a male captive by eating it.

The Shawnee and Noah's Flood?

The Shawnee creation story is very unique for the Algonquian group in that the Shawnee are the only tribe to believe they had crossed open waters at the time of creation. Also unique to them is the belief that a female deity, known as Our Grandmother, had created everything. The Shawnee believed in a supreme being known as Moneto, aka Great Spirit, who had the idea for creation. According to the Shawnee story, "In the beginning there was the Great Spirit, formed of wind, invisible, but in the shape of a man. He lived above the sun. There was just space; no earth, no water. The Great Spirit said, 'Let there be woman' and as soon as he spoke there was a being formed as a woman. Then to this woman the Great Spirit gave the work of creating this earth, light (the sun), water, people, and animals. She is the one the people saw and knew. Before the flood she and the devil and her grandson and the great giants were all on this earth, which she made, and the people talked to them. In this first creation, people lived along time and died four times, but not so today. The Great Spirit must have made the sky, or again it might mean that the Great Spirit was the sky. The female creator (Our Grandmother) is under the Great Spirit. Afterward the female creator did her creating and made the rules which are to be fulfilled."

According to George Bluejacket at Wapaughkonnetta on October 29, 1829 this is how the Shawnee had survived the great flood:

"The beginning of the Shawanoe tribe was when the Go-cum-tha (our grandmother) of our people come up out of the great salt water holding to the tail of the Ne-she-pe-she (Panther). Her Wash-et-che (Husband) was carried to the shore by a very big Wa-be-the (Swan or Goose)."

The land where their people had lived was swallowed up in the great salt water by Watch-e-men-e-toc (Bad Spirit or Devil), but Mish-e-me-ne-toc (The Great Spirit) saved these two and they were the first of our tribe. Many animals and birds were saved too, so there was plenty of hunting in the new Me-to-quegh-ke (Forest).This was many Te-pe-wa-ko-te (Hundred seasons or years) ago, and our people soon became many. They have always been called Shawanoes (Water people), and the Me-she-pe-she (Panther) and Wa-be-the (Swan) have always been the signs (Emblem or Totem) of this tribe."

Thirty years later, Charles Bluejacket, explained how both the white man and the red man were saved during Noah's flood. He said the white man and his family were in the great canoe that saved the white family, just as the Bible records. As stated above, a red woman had been saved as well. After the flood, Moneto, placed her in a valley with a hill between her and her white brother and his family. She could see the smoke from the white man's wigwam. Feeling quite lonely she wept. The Great Spirit came down. She told him she was just an old woman and she was the last of her people. He reminded her of how the first man had been created. After the Great Spirit had left her she began to form children out of clay. She tried to breathe life onto them but nothing worked. She wept. The Great Spirit once again visited her. She told them what had transpired. He once again reminded her of the story of the first men. After the Great Spirit left she breathed into the nostrils of her clay children and they became alive. This was the beginning of the red man. The people were one tribe and grew numerous.

The Iroquois Confederation

and

The Beaver Wars

It All Started With the Beavers

Native American groups had already been hunting beavers for their meat and furs by the time Europeans began to settle in North America. The North American fur trade market began with the Iroquois and European traders. Within a few years of Dutch, English and French arrivals they began to negotiate trade relations within the Mohawk Valley. During the 1620's the Dutch established several trading stations within the Hudson Valley and began trade relations with the Iroquois, especially the Mohawk.

The Iroquois wanted European trade goods such as iron tomahawks, brandy, rum, knives, axes, fish hooks, various colored clothes, woolen blankets, linens shirts, brass kettles, silver jewelry, assorted glass beads, guns and powder. The European traders desired beaver pelts to ship back to Europe. The land was plentiful with wildlife and the Iroquois didn't see a problem with paying for the items they desired with pelts. They not only hunted beavers but also mink, deer and fox. With each beaver pelt that had been sent back to Europe there was a greater demand for more. Slowly, the Iroquois began to depend upon the European trade goods. In order to assure trade between both parties, Iroquois elders would offer marriage between Iroquois woman and the traders. By the 1640's the Iroquois were fully armed with Dutch made firearms and were a force to be reckoned with. Due to the change of native technology and the demand for beaver furs, the beaver population which had once been prevalent in the Hudson valley had largely disappeared. Not only had the beavers declined but so had their own population through diseases such as smallpox. In order to save their livelihoods, the Iroquois turned their eyes upon New France.

The French and the Iroquois War

In New France, the French had understood the necessity of establishing trade relations with the native populations. They not only spent much time with the native populations but learned their language as well. Jesuit missionaries brought the Catholic faith to the natives. Native American groups throughout New France converted to the Catholic faith, lived in French mission villages, attended mass and wore crucifixes. The natives of New France had a monopoly on the lucrative French fur trade. Unlike the other tribes of the Iroquois Confederacy who had resisted the French, the Mohawk openly embraced the French way of life and Catholic religion. One Mohawk woman who converted to French Catholicism, Kateri Tekakwitha, is honored by the Catholic faith as the patroness of ecology, nature, and environment. Pope Benedict XVI has approved for the canonization of Kateri Tekakwitha into sainthood. You can read more about her life and conversion at http://conservation.catholic.org/kateri.htm

While the Mohawk's had already established trade with the French, the Seneca and other members of the confederacy feared the Wyandot and other Great Lake tribal nations were becoming too powerful with their ties to the French. They weren't the only ones who were noticing this. Nicholas Perrot wrote in the seventeenth century of the Great Lakes tribes possessed an "arrogant notion that the French cannot get along without them, and that we could not maintain ourselves in the Colony without the assistance they they give us." Backed by their English and Dutch allies, the Iroquois went to war against the French and their Native American allies. The Iroquois were relentless and ruthless. During the same time the Iroquois invaded French territory, a Smallpox epidemic had also spread among the villages. Too weak to fight back the Iroquois invaders many of the tribes and confederacies, such as the Erie, were decimated by the Iroquois.

While the Iroquois were battling the French along the Great Lakes region they also tried to expand their hunting territory into the Ohio wilderness. They soon came into contact with the most powerful tribe of the area, the Shawnee. During the seventeenth century the Shawnee were living in the Ohio Valley. When the Iroquois had begun to invade their lands, smallpox and other European diseases had already crept into the Shawnee villages. The Iroquois demanded the Shawnee to leave the Ohio Valley so they could hunt the beavers that were plentiful there. Not much is know about the Shawnee before or during the Beaver Wars. Too weak from disease and with the threat of decimation by the Iroquois, the Shawnee refused to fight their invaders. In order to save themselves the Shawnee split into five groups, most likely their five divisions, and left the Ohio Valley. The five groups spread into all different directions. One group went west to La Salle's post at Stand Rock (Fort Saint Louis) in Illinois. They remained there from 1683-1689. In 1680, a group of Shawnee who had made it present day Augusta, Georgia, evicted the Westo tribe from their homelands and made themselves the dominant tribe of the area. In the Carolina's a Shawnee group established trade relations with Carolinians who would regular supply them with slaves and guns. No matter where they went, the Shawnee would forcibly remove the native inhabitants of the area they wanted to settle in and then became the dominant tribe in that area.

Into the West: Conflicts with the Shawnee

The Shawnee Diaspora had an everlasting effect on the Shawnee. With their villages spread across vast amount of territory, the Shawnee adapted their lifestyle in order to stay in communication with other members of their tribe. They were known for their widespread migrations and settlements. The Shawnee would walk many miles in order to communicate with another tribes. Because of their vast territory many tribes learned the Shawnee language. This helped when the Shawnee were trying to gather forces against the Europeans. During the time of Iroquois occupation of the Ohio Valley, the Shawnee were able to still hunt upon the lands just not settle down in them. The Shawnee continued to hunt in their homelands thus never fully handing over control of the valley to the Iroquois. Despite this fact the Iroquois were quick to claim Ohio as their own by military conquest. They regarded any Delaware or Shawnee tribe still living in the area as dependents of the Iroquois Confederacy. In the mid eighteenth century the Iroquois had all but abandoned the Ohio Valley. The Shawnee began to return to their homelands after being away for nearly a century. Although they dwelt peacefully in the lands, the Iroquois still affect their lives. In 1768, the Iroquois sold the Ohio Valley to the British in Treaty of Stanwick, which allowed settlers to cross over into Ohio for colonization. The Shawnee and other Ohio Valley tribes never recognized the Treaty of Stanwick since they were not consulted in the matter. Any European who decided to hunt, explore or settle in the Ohio Valley were considered a threat by the Shawnee.

True Love's Kiss

Closing my eyes
I let my mind escape
Flying higher
I soar
Straight through the door
Of Evermore

With wings of fairies
Magic lifts me towards you
Songs of the lark
Guide me home
To a world I never want to depart

Friends merry met I long to see
Elves, fairies, unicorns and more
Alas my true love
Approaches me with his arms open wide
I run, oh how fast I run.
My heart beats fast as he holds me
How I have missed this prince of mine
He leans down and grants me
My true love's kiss.

Daniel Boone In Love

Known as Becky by her family and friends, Rebecca Ann Bryan was born on January 9, 1739 in Winchester, Fredrick County, Virginia to Joseph Bryan, Sr. There is no documentation of who her birth mother was. Some say her mother was Hester Hampton, who died in childbirth. Rebecca was raised by her father's second wife Alice (Aylee) Linville. The first ten years of her life she spent in Virginia. Like Daniel, her family was Quakers. In 1749, Rebecca and her father moved to the Yadkin River Valley of North Carolina with her grandfather. Her grandparents, Morgan and Martha Bryan were Quakers who had met on a voyage across the Atlantic Ocean bound for Pennsylvania. Morgan and Martha married, settled in Pennsylvania had seven children. Morgan and his family never joined a meetinghouse. After ten years of marriage, Morgan grew discontent with the restrictions and ostracism of Pennsylvania. He decided to move his family to Virginia in 1734. In her late sixties, Martha died in 1747. Two years later, when he was nearly eighty, Morgan led his married sons and daughters into the Yadkin Valley. Squire and Daniel Boone had already been hunting in the area as of 1750. Squire may have met Morgan and his family during this time. Two years later, Daniel and his family would move into the same valley.

After Squire Boone moved his family to the area, his family had become friends with the Bryan family. Daniel was five years older than Rebecca. He often went hunting with her older brothers. When the French and Indian War began, Daniel Boone left the valley to serve as a supply wagon driver and a blacksmith for the British commander General Edward Braddock. It was during his service with the Britsh that Boone met John Findley. The two men would become friends and later on explore Kentucky together. John had filled Daniel's head with dreams about Kentucky. After Braddock's defeat at the Battle of Monongahela, which Boone had barely escaped, Daniel went back home to his family with only one thing on his mind. Courtship.

Daniel had probably already heard about Rebecca from one of his many hunting trips with her brothers in his youth. When he had returned to the valley he was reminded of her again during the series of weddings. On the morning of any wedding, the men would gather, pass a jug of alcohol and roam the countryside urging the neighbors to attend the festivities. In 1753, there were two Boone-Bryan weddings. Daniel's younger sister, Mary, married Morgan's son, William. Daniel's sixteen-year-old sister thus became Rebecca's aunt. The two women were the same age.Since Rebecca's brothers had been in attendance it is likely Daniel heard stories about her from her rowdy brothers. Later that year, Daniel's brother John married Morgan's daughter, Rebecca. He became Rebecca's (Daniel's future wife) uncle. It was at this wedding that Rebecca and Daniel first took notice of each other. Daniel was smitten by her.

Legend says Daniel had first began courting Rebecca when one summer evening he had decided to go fire-hunting. Fire-hunting is when a hunter decides to hunt a night using only a torch as his means of light. Any deer who caught sight of the flames would freeze in fear and the light would reflect off of the deer's eyes. The eyes would then become the hunter's target. According to the legend, Rebecca was out in the night looking for stray cows when her own eyes had reflected Daniel's torch. He had no idea she wasn't a deer so he took aim upon her. Sensing something was wrong, Daniel held his fire and paid closer attention to his target. He notices the light coming off the eyes were different then he realized he was aiming at a person. Daniel held his aim long enough that Rebecca ran for her life. Daniel never again took up fire-hunting. When Daniel's family had first heard this story none of them believed it. One of Daniel's nephews once said the story was "Without foundation. As fabulous as it is absurd."

A second story of how Daniel and Rebecca had begun their courtship does not come from folktales but from his own family. The Bryan family was not of the same class as Daniel. Rebecca had come from a family who had money and land. Daniel's family did not fare so well. Daniel had decided to show Rebecca that he was a strong provider and hunter. As was the tradition of their time, Daniel had killed a deer then went to Rebecca's house with it. He stood outside her house, cleaned it then began to cook the meat over a fireplace. His shirt was still covered in the gore and blood from his butchering but he didn't care. Rebecca and her sisters found Daniel's gesture amusing and appalling. They laughed and made fun of him. Daniel had always been sensitive to criticism but he didn't let his hurt feelings stop him. Daniel ignored their taunts, picked up a cup to drink, peered inside it then remarked to them "You, like my hunting shirt, have missed many a good washing." The insult was meant to remind Rebecca her place. He wouldn't stand for a proud woman.

The two began courting in the summer of 1756. Romance did not play a large factor. It was more of a time of mutual testing to be certain they were right for each other. The couple had told the tale to their children about the first time they had been left alone together. They had been out cherry picking, a common thing for wooing couple to do together, when they had decided to sit underneath a cherry tree. Daniel had been in his hunting shirt and she wore a white apron, to show her domestic talents. Daniel was feeling uncomfortable. He halted their conversation, pulled out his hunting knife and cut several large gashes in her apron. He put his knife away and never apologizes, only waiting to see what her reaction would be. He once told his children he had done so "to try her temper." When she did not fly into a fiery rage he knew she was the right woman for him.

Daniel's father, Justice Squire Boone, married Daniel and Rebecca on August 14, 1756. There were two other couples married at the same time. After the wedding the couple joined in a feast that Rebecca's sisters had prepared for them and their guests. Usually the celebration would have been at the couple's home but since they had none of yet, they had to live with his parents. The celebrated lasted throughout the day with plenty of cider, rum, whiskey and food. All of Rebecca's belongings had been sprawled out so the guests could examine them. Since Rebecca came from the upper class she had brought with her a large amount of linens, furniture and cooking equipment. At mid-evening, as was the custom of their time, the bridegrooms and bridesmaids escorted Daniel and Rebecca to the bedroom. The attendants tucked them into bed then left to rejoin the party downstairs. Daniel and Rebecca consummated the union. As Rebecca lay underneath Daniel, they could hear the rude jokes and comments coming from underneath the floorboards. Nine months after the wedding, Rebecca gave Daniel a son they named James. She would give him nine more children - five sons and four daughters. Each child averaged only two and half years apart in age. On top of her own children she and Daniel also raised his two nephews, whom they had taken in as their own soon after the wedding. By the time Rebecca has turned twenty she was already rearing four children. Their marriage lasted fifty-seven years.

Love

Love is like the sun setting over a lake.
Love is like having a party with a big ole' cake.
Love is beautiful!

To Be or Not To Be

Elephant's roam fearing for their lives.
X-tinction is on their minds.
Tortoises tense while looking for food.
Insects scatter like rain on a roof.
Noble lions and lionesses hide in the brown grass.
Cheetahs run to save themselves.
Tigers roar their cry.
In the distance man walks._
Otters slide and dive.
Nearby the swans swim.

In a faraway land, giant pandas eat bamboo.
Squirrels gather up high.

Foxes as red as blood hide in their caves.
Ostriches bury their heads.
Rhinos run to save their young.
Everywhere man comes, animals hear.
Voices or sounds to make them fear.
Every animal knows when danger is near.
Running around, killing them is not what God would have wanted.

Bears

Brown and grizzly
You are the tower of strength
Filled with wisdom
That last for ages

Once man revered you
Loved you
Needed you
Sought you
But now you are just a shadow of our past

Once sacred by our forefather
No longer
Now you are only held precious as a Teddy Bear
Immortalized forever
Cute and cuddle
Laying on my dresser
Beckoning for a good night hug
Ready to defend me against the monsters
My most precious teddy bear

The Fishing Pole

A fishing pole is a curious thing
It's made of just a stick and a string
A girl at one end
And a wish on the other
To catch a fish for my supper

The Ever Elusive, Socks

Socks.
I should have named her Bandit.
For that is what she is.
She steals my pens and ponytail holders,
And sneaks into rooms like a spy.
Clank, I close the door.
Moments later everything in the closet hits the floor.
As slick as she may think she is.
I have trapped her.
Panic stricken and angry,
She leaps out of the closet when I open the door.
She is the queen of the castle,
Or so she believes.
Ask the dog or the other cat,
They may disagree.
Visitors? Forget it.
She doesn't play.
Hiding until they go away.

Funny

Horses make Horses
And ants make ants
Elephants make elephants
But bees make honey
Now isn't that funny?

The Basics Of Raising Rabbits

Adopting a rabbit can be exciting for anyone, especially a child. As a previous Holland Lop breeder I am often asked questions concerning the basic care of these wonderful animals. I hope this blog will answer those questions any new rabbit owner may have. A female rabbit is called a doe and a male rabbit is called a buck. A buck generally reaches sexual maturity at three months whereas a doe reaches maturity at six months. It is generally a good idea to separate bucks from any other rabbit, regardless of sex at this time.

Once the mother is pregnant she will carry her kits (the baby rabbits) for up to 33days. The kits are born deaf, blind and without fur. Generally, the litter will not survive for a first time mother. A doe has two uterus'. Each uterus can hold up to 7 kits. This means if she has been double inseminated by the buck she can have a maximum of 14 kits at once. Ten days after the kits have been born they will begin to open their eyes and their fur will begin to grow. Between two and three weeks of age they will begin to crawl out of the nest on their own. It generally takes the doe anywhere between four to six weeks to wean her babies completely. Once this had been accomplished the babies are removed from the mother's cage. We remove our Holland Lops at 4 weeks but do not adopt them out until they are 6 1/2 weeks old. This is to ensure they are healthy enough for adoption and to see if there are any we would want to keep as show rabbits. It is best for anyone who wants to adopt a rabbit not to do so before 5 weeks. Never let a breeder convince you to take a rabbit younger than this. Also be certain to ask the breeder if they are supplementing the rabbits diet with hormones. Unfortunately, there are some who do this to make a profit. This is dangerous to the animal.

Once you have your rabbit at home what do you do next? There are two areas a rabbit can live in. The first is a cage or hutch. The size of the cage or hutch depends on the size of your rabbit. There are many different types of hutches and cages out there. I use wire cages that have the litter pan on the bottom below the wire floor. I would highly suggest a cage with a litter pan. Rabbits are very sensitive and highly susceptible to infections if they walk in their waste. The rabbit must have enough room in the cage to stand up and run around. Reaching into the cage you may experience different reactions from the buck and the doe. Does are very territorial. Once inside their cage that is there home. Bucks will be more accepting of you reaching inside their cage. As I tell my customers, "They are the ADHD bunnies." Bucks are very curious and will want to explore everything, everywhere. After you have the cage, water bottle and food bowl place the rabbit inside. Rabbits cannot withstand heat 80degrees or above. So you will want to ensure they have access to an air conditioner or placed inside. They can die from heat stroke or dehydration.

Now what do you feed it? Rabbits have very sensitive stomachs. NEVER feed them cabbage or lettuce. These foods will get stuck in their digestive system and may lead to medical complications. Another thing to keep away from rabbits is Alfalfa. Alfalfa causes diarrhea in rabbits. A good hay treat is to use Timothy Hay. I feed our rabbits a handful every other day unless I have a pregnant doe. She gets more. Timothy Hay provides additional proteins that may be lacking in their diets. You will also want to supplement their diet with a salt wheel. As for main diet I would highly suggest Purina Show Rabbit Pellets.

Rabbits are very clean animals. Like a cat, they can be litter trained. I have had some customers who buy rabbits from us that allow their rabbits free roam around the house and train them to use a litter box. This is very simple to do. Rabbits, like rodents, have teeth that are constantly growing throughout their lives. It is highly recommended the new owner place a chew toy inside their cage. The best chew toys I have discovered is called K-Bob. You can buy these in the bird aisle at Petsmart or any other Pet Store. They are wooden blocks that hand down a metal cylinder. Sometimes you can place a salt wheel on these. Hang it inside the cage and the rabbit will play with it. Another item I highly recommend is a plastic cat ball. Rabbits love the sound it makes as they roll it across the cage.

Like any animal, rabbits are susceptible to a wide variety of diseases. There are resources on the web that will help you if you have concerns. The best advice I can give is to find a Vet that has expertise in rabbits. Unfortunately that is harder than it sounds. Rabbits are known as exotic pets. I would suggest, when trying to find a vet, call the ARBA. They have a list of vets across the country that have expertise in rabbits. You can find their number on their website at www.arba.net

Whether for show or as a pet, rabbits can be fun to raise. Enjoy your new friend.

The Waters of Life

The sea of life calls me by name
Up and down on the waves of life's experiences
Do I surf or drown in the complex waters of life

I swam the ocean waves alone until he came into my life
The dolphin, soaring through waves with ease
as if he was called from heaven to guide me home.
The experiences of life making him stronger
His view of the world focused solely on creator and lessons given to learn

He flips in the air
His sights on higher things
His creator, his friend and guide.

So many predators threating his existence
Yet he swims without a care in the world
Seeking companionship and friendship with his fellow dolphins
Enjoying a day of dance
His creator his only care in the world
The waters of life.

Kentucky's Hidden Gem: Rabbit Hash

Deep within the northern reaches of Boone County lies the hidden Kentucky gem of Rabbit Hash, Kentucky. One of the few early 19th century Ohio River towns left in America, Rabbit Hash maintains its eclectic charms. The United States Post Office built on January 3, 1879 originally deemed the village "Carleton, Kentucky." Yet residents soon found that many travelers mistake the village for Carrolton, Ky. Several stories abound concerning how Rabbit Hash received its name. Robert Rennerick, author of "Kentucky Place Names," retells an explanation A.M. Yearley wrote in his 1960 "History of Boone County." He writes of two salt or fur traders:

"During the flood of 1816, two travelers were looking for something to eat. When they asked about the availability of food they were told that because the flood drove so many rabbits into the hills, there were plenty of rabbits available to make hash."

Another version that took place thirty-two years before the post office changed the name of the town, stipulates that during the Christmas Day flood of 1847, due to two feet of snow combined with extreme cold, residents had to take shelter with their neighbors. With no food to eat and hunger rampant, they began to speak of the animals they would have hunted for Christmas Dinner. They spoke of geese, hens, and other animals. When they asked what Frank would have served, he simply replied, "Rabbit Hash."

One local resident told me the town was named after a local flood. The residents were starving. They looked to the Ohio River when they saw several dead rabbits floating on top. The residents had Rabbit Hash, thus the name stuck.

Whatever the reasoning behind the town's name, Rabbit Hash has enjoyed a cooperative relationship with its sister city across river. Built in 1813, Rabbit Hash sits upon the Kentucky shore across the Ohio River from Rising Sun, Indiana. Established in 1814, Rising Sun enjoyed the benefits of trans-river commerce. During the riverboat era, Rabbit Hash tried to conduct a port, yet due to sandbars and shallow water—so shallow you could cross the Ohio River by foot—the town abandoned their hopes. Riverboats made their way through Boone county with a stop at Rising Sun, Indiana. The cross-river traffic brought several benefits and amenities to Rabbit Hash, permanently connecting the two towns.

Like most towns on the Ohio River, Rabbit Hash has seen its fair share of flooding. Along the exterior wall of the mercantile building, flood gauges mark the height of each flood. Although I stand six feet tall, the flood of 1773 and another flood towered over my head. It serves not only a historical reminder to the dangers of building a town so close to the river but a gentle mark of heritage. Although Rabbit Hash is located 506.1 miles below Pittsburg, life along the Ohio River can be traumatic and peaceful for any resident or visitor.

Rabbit Hash General Store lies at the center of the historic town. The buildings surrounding the town contain a wide variety of antiques and oddities any collector would love. Due to the historical society proprietorship and marked National Register District, all buildings maintain their 18th century glamour. Although the buildings contain running water and electricity, nothing else is changed. You feel as if you've entered an early 19th century frontier Kentucky town. Built in 1831, the Rabbit Hash General Store hails as the oldest building on the 33-acre linear rural village. It contains several unique items, along with soft drinks, teas, and food items. The Rabbit Hash General Store has continuously been a working general store since its establishment.

My Kentucky Cabin

Darkness surrounds my little Kentucky cabin
Within the stillness of the night.
Candlelight illuminates the small area of my wooden table.
Drip.
Drop.
The wax falls down the pewter candleholder.
My left hand guides this feather pen of mine
along the precious brown paper.

The warmth of the fireplace behind me,
speaks words to my ears
Crackle.
Crackle.
The burning logs sing their songs.
Flames of red, blue, orange and yellow dance in the air.

I smell the aroma of fresh deer stew.
It boils gently in my copper kettle upon the metal arm over the fire.
Bubble.
Bubble.
It waits for my husband's return.

My children sleep in a loft above my head.
Snuggled deep in their blankets,
Warm for the night.
Snore. Snore.
The only sound I hear.

Alone with my fire, stew, paper, and feather pen
I secretly bid them all goodnight.

The Farmer's Market

We live in a world of consumerism, processed foods, and diets full of sugars and fats, while our fast-paced society is filled with overindulgence of material wealth and stressors that deteriorate our bodies. It is our diet that has led to the growth of obesity, eating disorders, and diabetes. Our diets have even threatened the lives of our children. Their sedentary lifestyle and diet have led to juvenile diabetes and obesity. The obesity has granted our children health problems that have generally not been seen in children but in adults. With our nation's health and children at risk, some families have turned to a change of diet and more active lifestyles.

A well-balanced diet of organic foods and healthier choices is hard to achieve in the United States. Our televisions bombard our children with advertisements for candy, soda, and fast food. Families with low incomes find it economically affordable to spend money on processed and fast foods. The market is saturated with subliminal messages promoting an unhealthy diet. It is less expensive to buy processed foods than healthy and organic ones. For a fast-paced society sometimes it is much easier and more cost effective to forego making meals at home and buy a value meal at your favorite fast food place. Many health conscious Americans have turned away from the supermarkets towards their local farmer's market.

A farmer's market often takes place outdoors. Local farmers generally gather with tables of locally grown and fresh products. Products may include homemade baked goods, jellies, meats, candies, vegetables, fruits, eggs, cheese, milk, and other products made on the farm. The small farmer depends on the farmer's market to make his products known to the public. By selling directly to the public he or she receives a better price than going through a middleman. The small farmer also plays a role in preserving not only America's agricultural legacy but its natural resources as well.

In today's agricultural society, major corporations such as Chiquita and Dole have saturated the market so much they have inevitably begun the decimation of small family-owned and operated farms. They buy large acres of land then reuse them every year instead of rotating their crops. Over time the overuse of the natural resources depletes the soil and the corporations must add chemicals to sustain their crops. They also use chemicals to repel pests. The corporate farmers depend upon the supermarkets and advertising to promote their products. Most of these products have been processed to sustain a longer shelf life. This process uses chemicals that are harmful to our bodies. None of the products sold at a farmer's market contains these chemicals.

Farmer's markets have developed over time across the entire United States. According to Wikipedia, the number of farm markets across the United States had grown from 1,755 in 1994 to 5,274 in 2009. Farmer's markets may be found in the large metropolis such as New York City down and small towns such as LaGrange, Kentucky. Food is not the only product available at a Farmer's Market. Artists, musicians, livestock, and crafts may be found as well. The duration and frequency of a Farmer's Market depends on the local environment in which one is established. Some take place during festivals while others are weekend events during the summer and fall. Travelers should never miss a Farmer's Market since they offer a realistic, localized flavor of the area.

Smart Couponing Saves Time and Money

Recently my husband and I have been trying to find ways to cut back on our expenses. We were intrigued by the show the "Extreme Couponers" how some families are able to walk out of a store with hundreds sometimes thousands of dollars of products and only pay less than $200 for each transaction. My husband and I are not alone. In our current economical times middle class families are hurting to put food on their tables while the rich get richer and the poor get poorer. So what is the average American family to do? Coupon.

My husband and I are by no means extreme couponers but we have found a way to lower our grocery bills, save on gas and help our soldiers overseas. Here are a few of our frugal tips.

How do I find enough coupons?

My husband and I do not live in a major city so it is useless for me to buy the local paper. Instead every Sunday I buy a copy of the *Courier-Journal* which is the local paper for Louisville Kentucky. Sometimes, if available I will also buy the Cincinnati paper. The only time I do not buy the paper is on holidays. Most newspapers will not place coupon inserts in their paper on the holidays. Sometimes though you can find the P&G insert which has valuable coupons for their brands. Buying a paper may give you only one copy of the coupon. I gain extra copies of the coupons I want by asking my friends to donate their inserts to me. **A lot of people will buy the Sunday paper only to throw these inserts in the trash.** I have known some people to dumpster dive for the thrown out inserts. I have never done this.

Three other valuable resources I utilize are coupon trains, a coupon groups and online couponing databases. A coupon train is like a nationwide coupon swap. The conductor (the person begins the train) places 50 coupons into an envelope and sends it off the first passenger on his or her list. The recipient (the passenger) can be anywhere in the United States. Once the train has been received, the passenger then sorts through the coupons. He or she takes out the expired ones. The passenger then decides which of the coupons left he or she wants and swaps out the old ones for ones they do not need. The train is sent on its way with still a total of 50 coupons to the next passenger. This process is called refueling. It continues along its route with each passenger conducting the same refueling process until it is sent home to the conductor. This is a wonderful resource because **not all coupon inserts are the same from coast to coast**.

Coupon groups are local groups where several couponers gather together once a week to swap out coupons. The leader of the group places his or her old coupons in a basket then passes it to the next member. Like the coupon train, that member goes through the stack, removes the ones he or she desire then replaces the missing ones with ones he or she doesn't want from his or her own personal stack. The member then passes the basket to the next person and the same process is repeated. This is also great because it allows members to share their own personal savings tips on a local level. Every store whether nationwide or not has localized sales.

Online coupon databases such as KouponKaren.com offer coupons that are not available in Sunday inserts. You can find almost anything in the databases for a variety of products and reductions. Coupons are updated daily and come from a wide variety of sources. These services are free for anyone to use.

So Now That I Have My Coupons What Do I Do?

Once I have my coupons it's time to sort them out. I have a large binder with plastic slips that are used to hold trading cards in. I keep all my coupons organized in that binder in alphabetical order. After I have placed my coupons in the binder I'm ready to start planning my shopping trip. The week of my trip I gather the advertisements for the stores I am going to use. I try to match my coupons with the items that are on sale. If I don't have that item I will utilize the online coupon database to see if I can get a coupon for that item. Most of my shopping trips are not for a single week. I have a pantry of items I try to keep stocked so if things are tight I can eat out of our pantry. Our pantry has also allowed us to donate food and items to local charities. You will want to build up your pantry as well. At first you may feel that this is insane but as you get use to it, it does pay off in the end. My husband and I have saved over $300 so far on our food bill and we've only been at this for a month. Most food items can last anywhere from three months to a year. I have found using a food storage guide helps me to keep track of how long an item can last. You can find these online.

Know Every Store You Shop At Like It Was The Back Of Your Hand.

Ah store policies. They have been in the news a lot lately. Some of the major chains are starting to change their coupon policies. What does this mean to the couponer? A lot. The coupon policy affects how the shopper will be able to use their coupons. Every store, whether a national chain or not, is different. Some stores allow you to use a store coupon and a manufactures coupon on the same item while others do not allow this. Some stores will double your coupons automatically and some you have to go on certain days. In order to save the most of your money it is best to stock up on your coupons until a sale hits. Then use all your coupons for that item at once with the sale price. But stores are starting to take notice of the tricks couponers use so you need to know up front what the stores expect from you. Make a list of the stores you use the most then call them to ask about their coupon policy. Some stores will direct you to an online policy while others may ask you come into the store so they can give it to you. Always read the policies carefully before you shop. Once you know what to expect you can plan your visit and become a more effective couponer. For example: Our local Kroger doubles any coupon 50 cents or lower everyday so I try to use that as much as possible. But they do not honor prices from other stores. Our local Walmart doesn't double coupons but will honor other store prices. Also for every $100 you spend at Kroger you can get 10cents off your next gasoline purchase. The $100 is the before coupon price. For example yesterday I went to Kroger and bought $48 worth of items for $12. Forty – eight points were credited to my gasoline points.

I Have Expired Coupons. What Do I Do?

Expired coupons are great! Never throw them out. Just because they are expired doesn't mean they can't be used elsewhere. Our soldiers overseas are able to use expired coupons six months after they have expired in the states. Every week I go through my coupons, pull out my expired ones and place them in an envelope. I then go online to my yahoo group, pick a station overseas and mail them to the family center of that base. Our soldiers appreciate these coupons more than you can know. It allows their families to save more money in a country where items may cost more than they do in the states.

Couponing is fun. You can be frugal and help another in need.

The Color of Hunger

Cold and confused in shades of grey,
my life's wasting away.
Rumble and growl.
My stomach complains.
Feed me.
But there's nothing more since last week.

For days I starved after the flood.
Once dependent upon my crops,
no more since the waters took it away.
My family died of disease.
Mosquitoes and other pests run rampant.
There's no escape,
from my terrible fate.

My mind plays tricks on me.
I savor for the taste of food.
Chicken, eggs, meat, and vegetables.
Their taste lingers on my tongue without substance.
Rich aromas of fire roasted food tickle my nose,
Yet I know they only exist in my mind.
I lie awake at night,
Afraid to sleep.
My dreams haunt me with food,
I can't prepare or taste in my own reality.
Frail, weak, and thin I dare not sleep.
Will I ever awake again?

The Candyman

A German immigrant, my grandfather, August Bruning, began his American business dream with his younger brother, Albert, during the early part of the 20th century, along the east coast. Bruning Brothers Confectionary ran for many years between New Jersey and New York, only to turn into Bruning Ice Cream in mid-century.

During the beginning of the twentieth century the local confectionary was the place to be for any youngster. Webster's dictionary defines a confection as any sweet food such as candy or pastry. A confectioner was the person who crafted the treat and his shop contained the most delicious treats he or she made from sugar. Today confectionary stores are hard to find in the United States. Some local and regional stores exist within small towns, yet commercialization has threatened these small business owners through supply and demand. Most of the modern day confections can be found anywhere from general stores to gas stations.

In the United States we call any confection candy. Yet travel around the world and you may encounter different names. For example, in Australia and New Zealand candy is often referred to as "lollies." Britain, Ireland, and other commonwealth states use the term "sweet." Confections come in a wide variety of categories. These include yet are not limited to: toffee, fudge, hard sweets, and licorice. While they taste good, moderation is best. Constant intake of any sweet may lead to type 2 diabetes or tooth decay.

In my grandfather's days, the supermarkets and convenience stores didn't exist for large candy makers, such as Hersey's, to market their products. Youngsters drove towards their local confectionary store to satisfy their sweet tooth. A trip into one of these stores was wonderland for any child. All types of candy displayed everywhere for the eye to see in a wide variety of color and imagination. I'm often reminded of the "Candy Man" from the 1971 movie "Willy Wonka and the Chocolate Factory" (my father, Roland Irving Bruning, loved that movie; so do I).

Throughout the 19th century, all candy had been sold to the consumer through loose small pieces that were weighed, bought, then bagged. In the early 20th century, the time of Bruning Brothers Confections, commercial confectionary stores grew rapidly across the

United States. Local confectionaries began to experiment with their own localized candy bar creations. Today some of these regional candy bars have become household names, such as Hersey and Mars.

I am proud of my grandfather who became a piece of American history as one of these confectionary owners. It's a shame the small town confectionaries have become a place of our past and not of our future as commercialization threatens our small town businesses. Next time you have a chance to visit a local confectionary store, remember men such as my grandfather who dared to dream of chocolate, sugar, fun, and children. The candyman.

Somewhere Out There

When I was little, I used to dream about the day I would reunite with my older brother. In 1986, a year after my father lost his battle to lung cancer, the song "Somewhere Out There" appeared in the movie *An American Tail.* In the movie Fieval and sister, Tanya, are separated. They sing the song together looking up at the moon dreaming of the day they would be reunited. Every time I heard the song, I dreamt Eric and I were staring up at the same moon dreaming of each other. I would crank up the volume and sing my little heart out with the dreams of my older brother.

Eric and I were born twenty years apart almost to the day. I was born January 22, 1976, in Cleveland, Ohio. Eric's mother died in 1979 and a year later our father married my mother. When I was four years old, my parents and I went to dad's WWII reunion in New Jersey. There dad reunited with Eric for a brief moment and told him he had a sister. I vaguely recall the union. That was the last time Eric saw dad alive. My parents divorced when I was six years old. Dad drifted in and out of my life for a few years. Then when I was eight, dad came back into my life and my parents started to talk of saving their marriage. By then it was too late, dad grew ill with lung cancer. I can recall the times he was well enough to speak to me. He told me, "Peanut, I'm going to beat this. Your mom and I are going to remarry. I made a lot of mistakes in my life but this time it's going to be different. We're going to be a family. We'll move to Florida and live on a houseboat close to your brother." Despite his best efforts, dad lost the fight in July of 1985, only a month after his sixtieth birthday. His dying wish for me was simple enough. Find Eric, tell him he died, he always loved him, and to give him some of dad's possessions. For twenty–six years I've searched for Eric and just when I had given up Eric entered into my life.

It's funny how just when you least expect it the impossible happens. I had given up on finding my brother for a couple of years. A piece of me was always missing. I felt a longing to find out more about my father's side of my family but I felt the pain too many times. Each time my hopes were raised they'd crash down. It was a vicious cycle that had to end or I'd go mad. My father's older brother died in 1997; after the funeral I called one of his daughters. It felt good to talk to her. I had hoped she knew where my brother was but the first thing she asked, "Do you know where Eric is?" I felt my hopes once again shatter. They hadn't heard from him in years. Determined I continued to search for him. I found Eric's law office, called him but his secretary never told him I had called. Once again, my heart broke. I was so close to him!

In 2001, I married the love of my life. I told him about my dad and missing brother. He urged me not to give up the fight. Last year, I searched the internet for any Eric James Bruning I could find. I knew his birthday, the state he lived in and that he was a lawyer. When I was little, dad had a picture of Eric with his wife. I use to stare at that picture so much I had memorized his face. With a mental image and facts stored in my mind, I searched MySpace, Facebook, and other social networks I could think of. Finally I found an Eric Bruning in Florida and sent him a message. A year went by with no reply. My heart fell again. Thoughts rolled in my head. Maybe he doesn't care he has a sister. I saved the picture of him he had on his MySpace account so I would have an updated photo of him. I thought to myself, he may not care about me but he's dad's son and I care a lot about him. I held that picture near and dear to my heart and vowed to end my search forever. Enough was enough.

Last year, I received an email stating Eric Bruning Refound You. I couldn't believe my eyes. Was this a joke? If it was, it was a cruel one! I read the email and my heart lifted a bit. I recognized the man in the picture. Eric was talking to me? Can this be real? I closed the email and looked through other emails he sent me. I read every single one. He told me details only he would know and left me a phone number. He wanted me to call! I picked up the phone and called him immediately. We've been talking ever since. My brother loves me and I love him.

The Folk In Backwatered Town And People

(Two poems in one)

The folk who live in backwatered town,
Tall people, short people
Are inside up and upside down.
Thin people, fat
They wear their hats inside their heads
A lady so dainty wearing a hat
And go to sleep below their beds.
Smart people, Dumb people
They only eat the apple peeling,
Man dressed in brown. Baby in a buggy
And take their walks on the ceiling!
These make a town.

Are You A Lake Person Or River Person?

Growing up in Ohio, my sense of direction was like most native buckeyes. When people would ask where I was from I would always reply, "Up by the lake." Anyone from Ohio could automatically assume I was from around Lake Erie. When I was sixteen, my mother and I moved from Ohio to Texas. My sense of direction was horrible. I had to learn to express myself as north, south, east, and west.

Four years ago, my hubby and I moved to Kentucky to be closer to my family in Ohio. A West Texas native, he quickly learned our culture was drastically different from his own. As soon as someone found out I was from Ohio they'd instantly ask me, "Where are you from?" I'd tell them up by the lake and sometimes they'd reply, "Oh, I'm from the river." My poor hubby would always ask "Oh, which river?" We would just laugh. You see, for any Ohio born and raised person we automatically assume the river is the Ohio River and the lake is Lake Erie. Now that I'm back in my own element I forget sometimes people don't understand Ohio sense of direction.

Ohio Directions
Up by the Lake = North
Down by the River = South
Over by Pennsylvania = East
Over by Indiana = West

Although we are from the same state, Lake and River people are completely different. I grew up close to the lake. There I was accustomed to severe storms. Lake people are used to harsh winters, occasional droughts, tornadoes, and the summer storms. Out on the plains when the thunder rolls it shakes the very earth you stand on and you feel its immense power deep within your soul. Lake people are used to large fishing boats, the ferries crossing to and from Canada, and the rich diversity of the growing cities. Below the lake, small farm towns fueled by railroads and industry dot along the plains.

I've lived close to the Ohio River for almost four years now. There's nothing like sitting on the river's edge and watching the coal barges pass you by. I love to watch Indiana drivers while I'm driving on the Kentucky side just parallel to me. On the lake I could never see to the other side. The river bridges fascinate me. I love being able to cross to a new state on a bridge. The only bridge I'd ever gone across a great lake was Mackinaw Bridge in Michigan and that's five miles long! River people are farmers. They're used to the rural country life with the occasional metropolis of Cincinnati, Louisville, and others. River folk know the power of an Ohio River flood. They've felt the disasters and learned to survive. They love to fish and boat in the river. I'm proud to say I was raised by the lake but now I'm a by the river person.

Oh, You're One Of Those Kinds Of People

Anthropology... When most people hear my background is in anthropology the first thing they think of is the atypical Indiana Jones type. To be quite honest, if Indiana Jones was alive today he would have long been criticized out of the anthropological community for his wanton destruction of the archaeological site he was supposed to be excavating. An no, archaeologists do not carry a whip around with them. They're not superheros fighting a great evil who wants to conquer the world, either. So then what exactly is anthropology? Anthropology is the scientific study of humans, past and present. While most people are familiar with archeology there are actually different fields encompassing the broad spectrum of anthropological studies.

1. These four fields are:
2. Biological Anthropology
3. Archaeology
4. Linguistic Anthropology
5. Cultural (social) Anthropology

Because humanity encompasses all four areas of anthropology, it is very common for anthropologists who work in one field of study to be exposed to another field while working on a project.
Biological or physical anthropology is further subdivided into primatology, paleoanthropology and contemporary human variation. As well-known primatologists you have probably heard of would be Jane Goddell. Her story can be found here: http://www.janegoodall.org/janes-story. Most primatologists also work to conserve the natural world. While primatologists study contemporary primates to learn more about the evolution of humans, paleoanthropologists utilize fossil remains to conduct their research. The third subdivision, contemporary human variation studies how human beings have continued to evolve. They seek to answer questions explaining the biological and behavioral differences of human beings in our world today. In the 19th and early 20th century, anthropologists would have used race to define a social

category of a person. This is no longer valid since it is widely accepted throughout anthropology that the biological makeup of a person has nothing to do with their behavior.

Archaeology

Most people I have encountered have often confused archaeology with paleontology. Paleontology is the study of non-human prehistoric life. So if you come a across a dinosaur bone don't call the archaeologist, call the paleontologist.

Archaeology also has its subdivisions, Prehistoric and Historical. The line between these two areas are drawn where writing began. Seems simple enough, right? Wrong. Not every culture developed writing at the same time. A historical archaeologists is only concerned with a society that has written records. While the prehistoric archaeologist is concerned with societies before they had the written records. Prehistoric archaeologists are further divided between Old World archaeology (Africa, Europe, and Asia) and New World archaeology (North, Central, and South America). You may have a historical archaeologist conducting research on a British colony in the New World, while at the same time a Prehistoric archaeologist is conducting research on a neighboring Native American village. Both are vital to each other in that they add to the cultural and historical record of that specific area.

Linguistic Anthropology

Can we say "Daniel Jackson?" Daniel Jackson is a character on Sci-Fi's hit drama *Stargate* played by Micheal Shanks. Jackson was a child of archaeologists who died when he was a child. Later in life he became an linguistic anthropologists who could speak 23 languages.

Linguistic anthropologists study how humans communicate with one another. Communication may be verbal or non-verbal. There are three sub fields; historical, descriptive and sociolinguistic. Historical linguistics studies how human language has changed over time and how each of those languages are related. Think about how easy it is for someone to learn Spanish after they know Latin or Portuguese but how difficult it is for someone who knows Spanish to learn German. That is because German and Spanish are not related. Descriptive linguists study how contemporary languages have changed from their original formal language. A good example of this would be the current change of language evident in American English. Many of our youth today are texting. Texting has broken down common formal American English words into a new code such as LOL (laugh out loud). Sociolinguists study all forms of communication (verbal and non-verbal) and how the social variation, social context and linguistic variations relate to one another.

Cultural Anthropology

This is my favorite field of anthropology! To understand cultural anthropology you must first know what culture is. Culture is defined as group of people's shared behaviors and beliefs. The United States is filled with many different cultures. One such group is the Amish. While most people think of the Amish as one group of people there are actually several different types of communities. What bonds each community together is their shared beliefs and behaviors. That is a culture. What they do may be different from what you do. You're culture is different from theirs. You live in the same country, though. This idea of shared land with many different cultures inhabiting it is nothing new to mankind. A cultural anthropologist will study a given culture for an extended amount of time by living within that culture. They are interested in examining how that culture is different and yet similar to other cultures of the world. Cultural anthropology asks us to think outside of our own culture and view a person from within their own.

So what does this all have to do with me?

Anthropology has everything to do with you! As a novelist sometimes I am asked to write from the point of view of a character that I do not share a cultural affiliation with. Understanding cultural anthropology has enriched my writing.

There are other careers out there that anthropology has been a vital asset to. A new field of study, known as applied anthropology, has guided many anthropologists to areas outside the anthropological discipline. Careers that utilize anthropology include Forensic Anthropologist (think CSI), Cultural Resource Management and non-profits among others.

The Old Man Of Pew

There once was an old man of Pew
Who dreamed he was eating his shoe.
He woke in the night,
In such a fright.
Only to find it was true!

Freedom At Last!

Graduation behind me
College before me
This one horse town beckons me to stay.
Freedom!
Oh, glorious freedom awaits me!
I've got to get out of here!

My parents are mad!
They expected more from me.
Expectations I could never meet.
Get married, settle down, and have a family of my own.
I don't want that.
I need my open space.

The world calls me
There're so many places I want to go,
People to meet
And things to do.
I can't list them all.

This small town is killing me.
My family yearns for me to stay
My heart says flee far, far away.
With eyes on the horizon
I pack my car.
Ready for a new adventure.

I am the wild one,
Independent and free.
I'm off to explore the brand new world
Never looking back
Always looking forward
For my next great adventure.
College here I come
Far, Far away from home.

Autumn Leaves

The autumn breeze sings a wonder song
deep within my soul.
A myriad of gold, red, and orange fill the countryside.
The woodland fairies dance with glee,
beckoning my curious heart.
"Sing and dance.
Rejoice with the bounties of harvest.
The time of closure draws near."

I stare upon the strong timbers.
Once mighty and full of life,
now her colorful leaves coast upon the gentle breeze.
Solid and barren she prepares for the cold winter.
No matter the hardships,
My tree friend shall withstand.
Such courage! Such strength!

Seasons come and go.
Our lives cyclical with new beginnings and old ways depart.
Ever changing, the world cries for my attention.
Listen, young one, Mother Earth cries.
Learn from the seasons of your life.
One door opens while another door closes.
With each passing moment of time
Wisdom waits for me.

Geocatching: A Modern Day Treasure Hunt

Technology plus hide and seek equals geocaching. With over 1,092,192 geocaches worldwide, geocaching entices adults to relieve their childhood in the wilderness. Adults from over 100 countries on all continents participate in the game. The game requires skills in benchmarking, trigpointing, orienteering, treasure-hunting, letterboxing, and waymarking. Equipment includes a GPS, waterproof container, logbook and a few small trinkets.

Invented on May 6, 2000 by Dace Ulmer of Beavercreek, Oregon the game continues to grow in popularity. A person who plays the game is known as a geocacher. The geocacher gathers a waterproof container, a logbook, pencil and a tradable trinket. Tradable trinkets ideas include books, unusual coinage, small toys, ornamental buttons, and CD's. Most trade objects do not hold high monetary values but are sentimental to the finder. Sometimes a cache may also contain a geocoin or travel bug.

These two objects, known to geocachers as hitchhikers, travel from one cache to another. Their exploits are available online. Never place food or something that smells inside the container. Stolen or vandalized geocaches are termed "muggled" or "plundered." "Muggles" are considered those who are unfamiliar with geocaching. Owners of the catch are responsible for maintaining the containers and objects. Waterproof containers may be as small as a finger to as large as five gallon buckets.

Once the geocacher has their treasures he or she chooses a location to bury their treasures. Locations may vary. Some geocache hiding places involve complex searches such as underwater, located 50 feet in a tree, staged multi caches, long off-road drives, high mountain peaks or in challenging environments. Urban environments also contain geocaches. Terms such as "drive-bys", "park 'n grab" and "cache and dash" refer to simpler geocaches.

Once placed in the ground the geocacher uploads the coordinates to the geocatching website. There are many geocaching websites worldwide. The largest geocaching website, Geocaching.com lists over 100,000,000 caches worldwide. Their free membership allows anyone access to geocaching locations. A paid, premium membership grants the geocacher extra search tools and member only geocache locations.

Finding a geocache can be as fun as burying one. On the website of their choice the geocacher locates a caches coordinates. They place the coordinators inside their GPS and begin their search. The search may leave lead to places they've never been before. Once the geocacher arrives to the cache's location reveal the container. They open the container, take out the logbook and sign it. Logbooks entries document who and where the geocacher came from and when the treasure was found. The geocacher then takes the trinket from the container only to replace it with a new one then reburies the cache. If a geocoin or travel bug accompanies the trinket they log into the site, placed the coordinates where it was found then bury it with their next geocache discovery.

A fun game with wonderful variations, the game creates controversy. Governmental and public opponents claim geocaching is only a collective effort to place more litter in the environment. In attempt to show otherwise, geochacers often travel with trash bags and pick up litter while searching. In 2005 South Carolina House of Representatives, in attempt to hinder geocaching, passed Bill 3777 stated, "It is unlawful for a person to engage in the activity of geocaching or letterboxing in a cemetery or in an historic or archeological site or property publicly identified by an historical marker without the express written consent of the owner or entity which oversees that cemetery site or property." The bill was sent to the Senate. The bill never left the Senate. Geocaching is legal in the United States.

It's Fair Time!

Keeping traditions alive
Everyone up here agrees
No one does it better than a good ole' state fair
Two weeks of non-stop thrills for all
Unfathomable shows of wonder
Cattle, donkeys, pigs, and more
Krispy Kreme donut burgers
Young and old from all over the state

Stay up late for a concert
Tables full of goodies
All the kinds of fun things to do
Tell me, oh please tell me, why are the kids in school?
Exhibits for 4H, Girl Scouts, and FFH

Fun days of adventure
All in one place
It's fair time
R we ready to do this again?

Ode To Camp Wakatomika

Oh, dear Camp Wakatomika
Do I ever miss you so
Every summer I had spent with you in my childhood

To walk the sacred trails
Other girls of long ago had tread

What fond memories I hold of you
Always beckoning me to walk in your woods
Keeping Girl Scout traditions alive
Always teaching me wilderness skills and more
Today, your camp is threatened to close
Oh how tragic still
My mind cannot even fathom nor
Imagine a world without a Gypsy campfire
Kapers, horseback riding, and more
All learned at Camp Wakatomika, the spirit of Girl Scout camping.

Hoppy's Grave at Camp Mowana, Ohio

Ohio has always been a mysterious land of myths and legends even before the white man ever crossed the Allegheny Mountains. The Iroquois named this land, Ohiyo, meaning "it is beautiful." The historic tribes of Ohio (Shawnee, Kickapoo, Iroquois, Mingo, Miami, and Delaware) often spoke of a mysterious tribe who had once inhabited the land and built the sacred mounds. Ohio is beautiful and mysterious. Drenched deep within its lands are myths and legends that span the ages. Unexplained happenings occur daily somewhere in Ohio. As a child I was very familiar with some of Ohio's paranormal happenings and found them fascinating. One of the stories I grew up with was the legend of Hoppy's Grave.

Hoppy's Grave

Deep within the woods of Camp Mowana located near Mansfield, Ohio lies the secret grave site of Hoppy. Long before anyone claimed the woodlands, Hoppy, a short hunchbacked hermit, lived by himself. No one ever knew where he had come from or how long he had lived in the wilderness by himself. Hoppy was a gentle soul who loved animals. They in turn loved him. He survived on his own, sleeping in caves, communing with the animals and depending on the wilderness. Even though the wilderness provides much to a man who knows the forest well, there are still supplies one cannot live without. Hoppy was no exception.

Ohio winters can be fierce. Each fall Hoppy made the long walk to Mansfield, Ohio. He gathered supplies he needed for the winter, exchanged pleasantries with the locals, then off he went into his wilderness home. At the melt of the snow, Hoppy returned to Mansfield, repeating his routine. This went on for years. Hoppy came and Hoppy went like clockwork. One fateful spring Hoppy never returned to Mansfield. Days turned into a week. The townspeople worried. It wasn't like Hoppy to never come into town after winter had ended. The concerned citizens quickly gathered together. Something was wrong.

They could feel it in their souls. The concerned townsfolk walked into the woodlands, desperate to find their little friend.

The search went on for an entire day. The people roamed every place they could think of. They searched the caves, the river, the woods and then just as they had almost given up hope of ever finding Hoppy, someone yelled, "I found him!" The search party gathered at the location. Hoppy's frozen body lay deep within a cave with his arms embraced around a fawn. He had laid his small body on top of the young deer, hoping to save it from the bitter cold, only to lose his own life in the end. Hoppy, friend of the forest, had tried everything he could think of to save the abandoned deer. Against all hopes, Hoppy failed. Both he and the deer had frozen to death. Heartbroken at the loss of their friend, the townspeople gathered Hoppy's body and buried him deep within his beloved forest. The following Spring the new trees near Hoppy's grave began to grow in an arch. Years passed. Each new and old tree bowed over and around his grave. Not a single tree to this day stands perfectly erect.

Over the years, the land where Hoppy's Grave and Cave stand have changed hands several times. Before the Evangelical Lutheran Church of America bought the land to create Camp Mowana, the camp had been a Boy Scout Camp. One day, a couple of boy scouts decided to hunt for Hoppy's Grave. Although the location of Hoppy's Grave has always been kept a secret, it isn't hard to miss if you know to look for the hunchbacked trees that surround the grave. The boys soon discovered the location in their wanderings. A large beehive hung off a branch from a tree that lay directly over the head of Hoppy's unmarked grave. The boys decided to see if the legend of Hoppy had been true. They knew that since it had been over fifty years since Hoppy had died his body would no longer be recognizable, but perhaps they could find his skeleton in the grave. The boys began to dig into Hoppy's grave. As soon they began, the bees within the beehive began to swarm at the boys. The boys ran as fast as they could. The bees gave chase until the boys had run far away from Hoppy's Grave, then the bees returned to their hive. The animals continue to protect Hoppy's grave to this day. If you ever visit Hoppy's Grave, you can be sure the animals are watching you. You too will face their wrath if you dare disturb Hoppy's Grave.

Hoppy's Grave, now resides within the Lutheran Camp Mowana.
http://www.lomocamps.org/camps/mowana

For generations, the story passed from counselor to camper to campers' children since 1941. To this day, the forest and animals continue to honor Hoppy.

Camp Mowana welcomes visitors as long as the camp is not in session. If you would like to visit Hoppy's Grave and Cave you can contact them at 1-419-589-7406. Camp Mowana is located on 186 acres of woods, streams, and Fleming Falls. Their address is 2276 Fleming Falls Road Mansfield, OH 44903.

Fleming Falls and the Ohio Valley Native Americans

Close to the cave where the residents of Mansfield found Hoppy is a small waterfall that leads out of Fleming Creek into a bottomless pond. Our legend this week takes up back in time to the early 19th century when settlers had begun to pour into Ohio. During this time there were several Native American groups in Ohio. The largest population being the Shawnee. Although the Shawnee are the most prevalent when speaking about Native American cultures in Ohio there are other groups worth mentioning who dwelt there too. Not all tribes were native to the region. As Europeans began to settle along the Eastern coastline the native populations were pushed westward. Five native groups relocated to the Ohio Valley during this time. These included the Miami, Delaware (Lenape), Ohio Seneca (Mingo), Ottawa and Wyandot. The Shawnee, Kickapoo and Erie tribes were bombarded not only with settlers but with these populations encroaching on their lands. With the greater population there was a larger demand on natural world to provide food, timber, and other needs. Not all tribes share the same belief systems as well. Some of these tribes fought against each other. It is during these turbulent times we find the Fleming family who settled along the Fleming Creek close to present day Mansfield, Ohio.

The Legend of Fleming Falls

On top of the smooth rock bed of Fleming Creek there once sat the mill and home of the Fleming family. The Fleming's mill was known for miles around to both natives and other settlers. A few years after they began their operation the Flemings became friends with a neighboring Native American village. Every year the chief of the village would visit upon the family and trade for their flour. Both the villagers and the family enjoyed the friendships. The Native Americans would even protect the Fleming's from other tribes who wished to do harm to the settlers. In return, the Fleming's agreed never to trade with the friendly village's enemies. The pact between the two had been kept for years and peace came to the Fleming's home.

The enemy tribe soon became jealous of the village. They wanted the flour too but knew the Fleming's would never sell it to them. The Fleming family was not only honest but loyal to the other village. The enemy chief decided if he can't persuade the Fleming's to give his village the flour then perhaps he could convince the other chief that the Fleming's had betrayed them. They were after all white people. All natives knew you could never trust a white person. White people speak with the forked tongue of the evil serpent. So he went the friendly village's chief with a peace offering. He told the friendly chief his village had been able to make it through the winter because the Fleming's had sold them flour. Enraged that the family would betray them the friendly village's chief went with a war party to the Fleming's mill. The family went out to meet their friends only to be met with hostility. The natives captured the family and demanded an explanation. Mr. Fleming denied ever selling the flour to the enemy village but the chief didn't believe him. He ordered the warriors to kill him and his family for betraying them. After the family was brutally executed the natives threw their bodies over the waterfalls then burned the mill and home.

A winter passed. Word had spread fast to all the tribes of what had happened to the Flemings. That spring, the enemy chief went to the friendly chief and confessed he had lied to them about the Flemings. He told the friendly chief he had never expected him to kill his friends. He only wanted the Flemings to be released from their agreement so other villages, including his own, could buy flour from them. Saddened by his grievous mistake, the friendly chief recalled the family's pleas. The family has spoken in truth and he had ordered the execution of innocent blood. The chief and his warriors went back to the creek where the mill and home once lay. They searched the pond for the family's bodies so they could be properly buried in the native ways. The deeper the warriors the dove the farther the bottom of the pond went. They dove until they could dive no more. Unable to find the bottom of the pond and the family's bodies, the natives asked for forgiveness in a ceremony on the site where the mill used to stand. Afterwards, they carved faces into the smooth bed rock and boulders around the site as a memorial. Every time it rains the faces cry showing the eternal sadness the chief and his warriors felt. If you go to Fleming Falls, the faces are hard to find. You can still see the imprints in the smooth rock bed of the creek where the mill and the home use to stand.

And the bottomless pond? During the middle of the 20th century, a woman once dropped her purse into the pond. Everyone who knew the story of Fleming Falls had warned her that the pond was bottomless and dangerous. Divers had tried to dive into it to retrieve it but was unable to find the bottom of the pond. It seems the natives were right. The pond at the bottom of Fleming Falls is truly bottomless. A boardwalk has been built for hikers to walk around the pond. It is not advised anyone should stray off the boardwalk to explore the bottom of the falls, least you fall in and never be heard from again. I often wonder what else is down there other than the Fleming family and the purse? What do you think?

The Mysterious Great Serpent Mound

Long before Europeans ever knew of the Western Hemisphere, Prehistoric Native American groups known as the Moundbuilders roamed the Ohio wilderness. These groups were named Moundbuilders after the earthen mounds they created. These mounds were created in a wide variety of shapes including conical, circular and animal effigies. When Europeans first explored this area they were shocked to see the numerous mounds dotting the wilderness. Today most of these mounds are no longer among us. Most of them have been destroyed by farming. Archaeologists struggle in a race to save what little mounds still dot the Ohio Valley. The largest animal effigy known to man is the Serpent Mound (aka: Alligator Mound) located near Peebles in Adams County, Ohio.

Serpent Mound measures 1330 feet in length with its height measuring three feet. It lies on top of a 100 foot bluff overlooking Brush Creek. Several caves lie underneath the bluff. It was known to many historical Native American tribes and early settlers. In 1846, it was first surveyed by explorers Ephraim Squire and Edwin Davis who documented the mound extensively. Forty - one years later Professor Fredrick Putnum acquired the land from the farmer who owned with the goal of preserving it. The farmer had already sold most of the land in the area allowing for the destruction of many other mounds that had surrounded the Serpent Mound. Fredrick Putnum conducted archaeological excavations upon the Serpent Mound and surrounding area between the years 1887-1889. Putnum discovered several mounds and graves within the area. He accredited the Serpent Mounds' construction to the Adena people. He based his belief on the findings of three Adena mounds and village near the Serpent Mound. Yet he never recovered artifacts from the Serpent Mound to correlate the Adena mounds to the Serpent Mound. In 1990 and 1992 Archaeologist Brad Lepper conducted his own excavations into the Adena village Putnum has discovered. Upon examining features with ceramics and flint tools, Leper determined the village was not an Adena village but a Fort Ancient one. He took charcoal samples from inside the Serpent Mound.

Radiocarbon dating revealed the mound was built around 1070AD. That would mean the Serpent Mound was constructed after the Adena people and during the time the Fort Ancient occupied the lands. Serpent Mound is located in the Ohio Historical Society Park and maintained by the Arc of Appalachia Preserve System. The park contains a museum, hiking trails, Native American village, and picnic areas. They are closed during the winter season. Hours vary by season. Admission is $7 per car. More travel information can be viewed at http://ohsweb.ohiohistory.org/places/sw16/index.shtml

Have We Forgotten?

Pack the car, its Memorial Day weekend. Families all over the United States begin their summer vacations. State, county and federal parks exploded with visitors. Small towns celebrate with festivals. Campgrounds fill. Friends and family open their grill for the big backyard barbeque. But wait, is that why we celebrate Memorial Day? What is Memorial Day?

Between the years 1861 to 1865 the United States of American fought the Civil War. The bloodiest war fought in America, the war tore families apart. Nearly 1,100,000 men suffered casualties and more than 620,000 lost their lives. More than 10,000 wartime battles occurred, many of them claiming lives on both sides. By 1865, women of Mississippi, South Carolina and Virginia decorated the graves of fallen soldiers. The following year, members of a Columbus, Mississippi women's memorial association, lay flowers upon both Confederate and Union graves. The humble actions of the southern women never went unnoticed. Poet Francis Miles Finch wrote of their deeds in his poem "The Blue and the Grey" published in the *Atlantic Monthly.* An editorial piece in the *New York Tribune* commented on the women's actions as well. Songwriter, Mrs. L. Nella Sweet dedicated her 1867, *Kneel Where Our Loved Ones Lay Sleeping* to the Southern women.

General John Logan, national commander of the Grand Army of the Republic, ordered the establishment of Memorial Day on May 5, 1868. First observed, May 30, 1868, families, following the southern women's traditions, strew flowers upon their loved ones graves at the Arlington National Cemetery. By 1890, all states, except the south, accepted Memorial Day. The South would not unify with the North in honoring the dead on May 30th until after WWII. The unification of honoring the fallen also expanded to any soldier of any war. Some southern states celebrate not only a national memorial day but have added a state memorial day to honor their fallen Confederate soldiers.

Another tradition to the holiday was added in 1915, when Moina Michael wrote,

"We cherish too, the Poppy red
That grows on fields where valor led,
It seems to signal to the skies

That blood of heroes never dies."

The red poppy, worn on the chest, came to symbolize the blood the fallen had shed. By 1924, the VFW began to sell artificial red poppies. Mrs. Michael was honored in 1948, with her image on a United States stamp. Every year, since 1951, Cub and Boy Scouts of America of Saint Louis, visit Jefferson Barracks National Cemetery only to place flags on 150,000 graves. During the late 1950's, soldiers of the 3rd U.S. Infantry placed flags at the head of more than 260,000 gravestones in Arlington National Cemetery. They ensure each small flag stands while patrolling the area 24 hours. In 1971, the United States Congress passed the National Holiday Act of 1971. The act solidified Memorial Day as a national holiday to be celebrated on the last Monday of May, allowing for a three day Federal holiday weekend. In 1998, the Girl and Boy Scouts joined the continued efforts. Each year, they place flags upon 15,300 gravesites located at Fredericksburg and Spotsylvania National Memorial. Washington D.C. reinstated the Memorial Day Parade in 2004. Unfortunately, while soldiers buried within National Cemeteries receive attention many city and town cemeteries do not. We must remember that our soldiers fight for our freedom. Will we honor them when they are gone? Or shall their graves be left cold without a person who remembers the sacrifice they gave?

Old Glory

Oh say can you see…
The beauty of the red, white, and blue
She waves proudly over the land
Announcing to all
America has withstood
When no one said she would.

By the dawn's early light…
Though tattered and torn
Old Glory waves in triumph
A symbol of freedom
Battered and bruised
Our soldiers cry our victory!

'Cause the flag still stands for freedom…
Those fireworks above her proclaim
Bursting with color
Like bombs lit in the night
Recalling the battles fought
The lives lost
And the freedoms our soldiers protect.

I'm proud to be an American
Where my forefathers sacrificed all
When I think of my patriot
Words cannot express my heartfelt gratitude
What fears he must have had to know he faced an impossible task
In order that I and future generations would have a better life
So let those fireworks burst
Let Old Glory fly
Sing the songs and never forget

My country, 'tis of Thee,
Sweet Land of Liberty

The Red, White and Blue Is Here to Stay

She flies high above our heads as she yells, "American I am, where do you stand? You who long for freedom, where do your loyalties lie?" On July 4, 1776 our forefathers declared the unification of the thirteen states free from England's rule. Often referred, the "First National Flag", American forces fought under the "Grand Union Flag" during the early portions of the Revolutionary War. Never officially recognized, the "Grand Union Flag" served a design template for Betsy Ross' American flag. On June 4, 1774, the newly formed nation adopted the American flag designed and sewed by Betsy Ross.

Her original flag contained thirteen stripes alternating red and white. A navy blue square situated on the upper left hand corner contained a circle of white stars, representing each state within the union. . In 1795, the United States added two new stars and stripes to their standards, representing the addition of Kentucky and Vermont into union. United States Congress continued to pass several acts concerning the national flag until 1960, when Hawaii and Alaska were added to the union.

The star designs over the years have seen many modifications yet the overall symbolic elements of the flag remain the same. Each color on the flag and symbolic design represents a different patriotic element. Red, the color of blood, represents the bloodshed on our battlefields. It is the blood of those who died and were injured in battle we must never forget. The brave men and women fought for to defend our rights and liberties. If not for our revolutionary heroes and the warriors who came after them we would not enjoy our freedoms. Their hardiness and valor shall forever remain in the red of our flag. Lest we forget the reason our ancestors fought the Revolutionary War, white the color of freedom, purity and innocence. Let us never forget the women and children who stand behind and support the troops; our friends, family and loved ones. Together we stand one nation under God. Blue represents vigilance, perseverance, and justice. We persevere to protect our equal rights. Our citizens vigilantly oversee our leaders. Our governmental leaders enact their decisions for the people by the people. The thirteen stripes remind us of those brave first colonies who stood small against a giant power. Through their bloodshed, determination, honor and vigilance they defeated the British and began a new country. Each star represents every states unified under our central government.

In the days of political correctness, information overload and political abuse I think of our founding forefathers. Those brave men and women struggled to start this great nation yet many of our citizens have long forgotten why the United States of America exists. They no longer honor the flag or other patriotic symbols. Our pledge becomes mundane. I know if our forefathers walked among us they'd scream "Have you forgotten!"

"We hold these truths to be self-evident, that all men are created equal, that they are endowed by their Creator with certain unalienable rights, that among these are life, liberty and the pursuit of happiness. That to secure these rights, governments are instituted among men, deriving their just powers from the consent of the governed." – Declaration of Independence

The American Flag. She flies proudly above the United States reminding us all, united we stand, divided we fall.

The Appalachian Irish

My Appalachian story derived from my great grandmother, Stella Virginia McCardle. Born and raised in West Virginia, she was the daughter of Appalachia Irish. The Appalachian Irish call themselves Scot-Irish to set them apart from their Irish-Catholic counterparts. It can be confusing to anyone in England, Ireland and Scotland to hear the term used because most of the Scot-Irish of America have any Scottish background. The Scot-Irish claim the term Scot in their cultural identity because their settlements inherited a Scottish flavor from their time spent at Ulster Plantation. Most of the Scot-Irish are descended from the Ulster Irish who emigrated from the Plantation of Ulster in the 17th century. They settled in the Appalachia Mountains to create a new home where they could worship freely without the persecutions they faced in Ireland from the Catholics.

The Scot-Irish originally referred to themselves as Irish until a century later when the United States saw a huge immigration of Irish during the Great Irish Famine of 1840's. Hundreds of families fled the Ireland during the great disaster, most of whom were Irish Catholic. The Irish Catholics preferred to settle in larger cities of Boston, New York or Chicago while the Scot-Irish stayed in the mountains. Yet what little interaction the two groups had with one another often lead to heated arguments. The Scot-Irish didn't want to be associated with the new groups. In response they began to use the name Scot-Irish to set themselves apart.

The Scot-Irish of America have a proud heritage that contributed to American culture. Cultural attributes included individualism, ruggedness, Indian fighters and a large anti-British sentiment. It was these attributes that led them to contribute to the fight for American freedom. During the Revolutionary War, one quarter of American troops were Scot-Irish. They often spoke Gaelic in their ranks. General George Washington stated, "If defeated everywhere else, I will make my stand for liberty, among the Scots-Irish in my native Virginia." President William McKinley said, "The Scots-Irish were the first to proclaim for freedom in these United States; even before Lexington Scots-Irish blood had been shed for American freedom. In the forefront of every battle was seen their burnished mail and in the retreat was heard their voice of constancy". A hundred years after the Revolutionary War, the

Scot Irish made themselves known in the Civil War. They have continued to fight for our freedoms since.

Father's Day: History In The Making

Father's Day Around the World

Father's Day has been traditionally celebrated throughout the world for over 4,000 years yet officially did not become a national holiday in the United States until 1972 . The tradition of celebrating Father's Day began in Babylon 4,000 years ago when a boy named Elmusu created a card made of clay for his father. In it he wished his father good health and long life. Today, we do not know what happened to neither him nor his father.

Countries from around the world traditionally celebrate Father's Day, along with the United States, on the third Sunday of June. Yet those countries where the Catholic Church is prevalent celebrate Father's Day on the Saint Joseph's Day, March 19. Recently, a new trend has begun in the countries that are heavily influenced by the Catholic Church. Secular celebrations have begun to appear without any religious associations. This means in those countries Father's Day is often celebrated twice, once on Saint Joseph's Day and again on Father's Day. The manner in which a country celebrates Father's Day varies from country to country. In Australia, families celebrate the holiday privately with a breakfast meeting with the entire family. South Africans often have picnics, go fishing or enjoy a meal at a restaurant with their fathers. Irish children, whose fathers have passed on, give donations or perform acts of service in their father's name. Several cultural organizations and clubs have special programs for Father's Day emphasizing the important role a father plays in a child's life. In Canada, children of all ages wear either a red rose, showing their father is still alive, or a white rose, showing their father has passed on, in honor of their fathers. Homemade cards, candies and other goodies are often given to fathers throughout the world. While Father's Day has become increasingly commercialized throughout the United States, one thing remains a constant throughout all nations. Father's Day is the day to honor the men who have dedicated their lives to their children. Any man who had held a fatherly role in a child's life is honored whether it be a brother, uncle, step-father, father, grandfather, foster father or a male mentor. Spending time with their father is a universal theme in celebrating Father's Day.

So how did the United States nationally come to celebrate Father's Day? There were many attempts throughout the United States to commemorate a day to honor fathers yet no one paid attention to these localized events for one reason or another. One such event was held on July 5, 1908 at the Central United Methodist Church in Fairfax, Virginia after the Monongah Mining Explosion of December 1907 left around a thousand children fatherless. Grace Golden Clayton whose own father, a Methodist minister, had been killed in the explosion organized a service to honor all fathers. She chose the date July 5th because it was the Sunday closest to her father's birthday. Despite all her hard work she had very little results. Word of the event never left Fairfax due to too many other events happening at the same time, too many people in the city and not promoting it outside Fairfax. It wouldn't be until 1910 when a widower's daughter named Sonora Louise Smart Dodd organized a campaign for Father's Day to be recognized that the United States would take notice.

The Widower's Daughter

Sonora Louise Smart was the daughter of the Civil War veteran William Jackson Smart and his wife, Ellen Victoria Cheek Smart. She was born on February 18, 1882 in Jinny Lind, Sebastian County, Arkansas. When she was nine years old, her family moved west to settle on a farm between Wilber and Creston in Eastern Washington State. It was here her mother died giving birth to Sonora's youngest brother when Sonora was sixteen years old, leaving Sonora's father to rise five children and an infant son by himself. A year after the loss of her mother, Sonora married John Bruce Dodd on November 4, 1899. On October 24, 1909, Sonora gave birth to John Bruce Dodd, Jr.

It was during her pregnancy that Sonora began to realize how many selfless sacrifices her father must have made to raise her and her siblings on his own. While she was listening to a Mother's Day sermon given by Reverend Dr. Henry Rasmussen at Central United Methodist Church in Spokane, Washington Sonora began to wonder why as a nation do we not honor our fathers. Her father had been loving, devoted to his children, strict, very caring and disciplined. Didn't he along with all the other fathers in this country deserve to be recognized as well? After the sermon she had told the pastor, "I like everything you have said about motherhood. But somehow, 'father' seems something apart. Do you not think it would be fair and fine to give father a place in the sun?"

Sonora had the vision and now she needed to make her dream a reality. She received her inspiration from Mrs. Anna Jarvas' efforts to make Mother's Day a national holiday. If Mrs. Jarvas could succeed in her cause then why couldn't she? In order to make Father's Day a state recognized holiday she would need to present a petition. It wasn't going to be easy. In her day in age women didn't get involved in politics let alone work outside the home. Gaining the support she needed to win a day set aside just for fathers would be next to impossible. She had once said it had taken a "certain degree of temerity". No matter how hard it seemed Sonora never gave up the fight. She rigorously fought for a national Father's Day by contacting local churches, the Spokane Ministerial Alliance, shopkeepers, government officials and the YMCA. Finally Mark H. Wheeler and George A. Forbes of the Spokane YMCA co-signed her petition. The three of them went to the Spokane Ministerial Alliance and suggested a date. Sonora had suggested they hold the service on June 5th, her father's birthday. Due to time constraints the alliance did not feel they had enough time to plan a well enough sermon for the 5th so they moved the event to June 19th.

On June 19th, 1910, the entire city of Spokane celebrated the first Father's Day. The Spokane Daily Chronicle placed an article on the front page of their June 6, 1910 edition stating, the Spokane Ministerial Alliance and the YMCA "enthusiastically" supported Sonora's proposition and declared June 19th Father's Day. Reverend Dr. Conrad Bluhm delivered the very first sermon at Sonora's church, Old Centenary Presbyterian Church. Other ministers from the area including pastors at the First Presbyterian Church and Central United Methodist Church gave Father's Day sermons as well. Both the mayor of Spokane and the Governor of Washington proclaimed June 19th as Father's Day. Washington was the first to celebrate Father's Day statewide. Roses of red and white were passed out to attendees as the Old Centenary Presbyterian Church. Sonora and her infant son traveled throughout the city in a two horse carriage delivering presents to shut-in fathers. Local papers took out ads with Father's Day themes. Children gave presents to their fathers. The press soon got wind of the large celebration. Seven national newspapers covered the event and the news spread nationwide about Father's Day. Afterwards Sonora received over 100 letters thanking her for suggesting a Father's Day.

She had tried to reply to all of them but soon found she needed help from her friends.

Father's Day continued to be celebrated yearly afterwards. The popularity of celebrating Father's Day slowly spread across our nation but was not federally recognized. Politicians and presidents informally supported the idea of Father's Day. By 1925, Father's Day was being celebrated in every state. The International Father's Day Association, of whom Sonora was honorary president of, decided in 1938 to never rest until congress officially recognized the holiday. In 1966, President Lyndon B Johnson signed a proclamation declaring the third Sunday of June Father's Day. It wasn't recognized by Congress yet, but it was a start. President Johnson ordered all the flags on government building to be flown at half-mast in honor of all United States fathers. Father's Day did not become a federally recognized holiday until 1972. In 1970, the joint houses of Congress passed a joint resolution declaring Father's Day a national holiday. Two years later, President Richard M. Nixon signed the proclamation making the third Sunday of June Father's Day's official destination and a national holiday. He invited all citizens to honor their fathers with celebrations. Father's Day has been nationally celebrated ever since. Sonora, now ninety, remarked "I am happy that this could have come to pass in my lifetime." The mother of Father's Day died on March 22, 1978 at the age of ninety-six years old. She is buried at Greenwood Memorial Terrance in Spokane, Washington.

Balance

Streets are crowded
Homeless surround us
Robbers rob us
Murders happen
Hate is having a heyday

Yet...

The sun is shining
Grass is growing
Children play
Lovers love
God is giving.

ABOUT THE AUTHOR

Bestselling author, screenwriter, blogger, and owner of Mountain Springs Publishing House, Allison Bruning has had a passion for writing since childhood. Born and raised in Marion, Ohio, currently she lives in Louisville, Kentucky with her husband, Delfin, and their Australian Cattle Dog, Lakota Sioux. Her father, Roland Irving Bruning was the son of a German family who immigrated to the United States at the turn of the twentieth century. Her mother's family immigrated from Scotland, Ireland, and England during the seventeenth century. Allison is a member of the Daughters of the American Revolution, tracing her lineage to the American Patriot, Private Rueben Messenger of Connecticut.

Her educational background includes a Bachelor of Arts in theatre arts with a minor in anthropology, and a Texas Elementary Teaching certificate, both acquired at Sul Ross State University in Alpine, Texas. While at Sul Ross State, she received National Honor Society membership in both programs of study, as well as admission to the All American Scholars register. She holds graduate hours in cultural anthropology and in education. Allison is currently working toward a Masters of Fine Arts in creative writing at Full Sail University in Winter Park, Florida, with a 4.0 grade point average.

She is also the recipient of the Girl Scouts Silver and Gold Awards.

In addition to family stories, history, especially Ohio Valley history, genealogy, and cultural anthropology, Allison enjoys traveling, camping, hiking, backpacking, and spending time with her family.

She can be found on Facebook at https://www.facebook.com/AllisonBruning. She is also on twitter @emeraldkell. Her blog can be found at http://allisonbruning.blogspot.com. Her author page on Goodreads is http://www.goodreads.com/emeraldkell and her Amazon author page may be found at http://amzn.to/LZ0UsT

www.ingramcontent.com/pod-product-compliance
Lightning Source LLC
La Vergne TN
LVHW091642100826
845152LV00006B/134/J

* 9 7 8 1 9 4 0 0 2 2 0 7 9 *